SOVIET EDUCATION: THE GIFTED AND THE HANDICAPPED

SOVIET EDUCATION
The Gifted and the Handicapped

EDITED BY
JIM RIORDAN

ROUTLEDGE
London and New York

First published in 1988 by
Routledge
11 New Fetter Lane, London EC4P 4EE
29 West 35th Street, New York NY 10001

© 1988 J. Riordan

Printed in Great Britain by
Billing & Sons Ltd, Worcester

British Library Cataloguing in Publication Data

Soviet education : the gifted and the
  handicapped.
  1. Soviet Union. Special education
  I. Riordan, James, *1936–*
371.9'0947
  ISBN 0-415-00574-4

Library of Congress Cataloging-in-Publication Data

ISBN 0-415-00574-4

CONTENTS

THE CONTRIBUTORS

The team of seven contributors comprises educational specialists and scholars with an interest in Soviet education. All are Russian-speakers who have made study visits to the Soviet Union; some have lived there for prolonged periods.

George Avis is Chairman of Russian and Senior Lecturer in Russian Studies at the University of Bradford; he is editor of The Making of the Soviet Citizen (Croom Helm, London, 1987).

John Dunstan is Senior Lecturer in Russian Studies in the Centre for Russian and East European Studies at the University of Birmingham; he is author of Paths to Excellence and the Soviet School (NFER Publishing Company, Windsor, 1978) and editor of Soviet Education under Scrutiny (Jordanhill College Publications, Glasgow, 1987).

Mike Lambert is Project Director of the Birmingham Institute for Conductive Education at the University of Birmingham; he was previously senior teacher at the Victoria School for Handicapped Children in Birmingham.

James Muckle is Lecturer in Education at the University of Nottingham; he was previously teacher of Russian at Leeds Grammar School.

Jim Riordan is Professor of Russian Studies at the University of Bradford and author of Sport in Soviet Society (Cambridge University Press, London, 1977).

Avril Suddaby is Lecturer in Business Studies at Merton College, London.

Andrew Sutton is Director of the Foundation for Conductive Education; he was previously Psychologist to the Parent and Child Centre in Birmingham.

ACKNOWLEDGEMENTS

The editor would like to express gratitude to the Leverhulme Trust and Bradford University Modern Languages Research Committee for their generous support of this project.

INTRODUCTION

Jim Riordan

In attempting to explain Soviet special education, we started out with two simple questions. What are the provisions for the gifted and the handicapped? And why are they made? In establishing the current situation and its underlying philosophy, however, we uncovered vehement controversies and debate about future trends among Soviet specialists, teachers, parents and students. Today, for the first time since the 1920s, the whole of Soviet education and society is in flux. Mikhail Gorbachov has called it a revolution, since 'the education system has in many respects fallen short of today's requirements.' (1)

We could not therefore rest content with catching a glimpse of the fleeting moment; such a view would be as unbalanced as it was unjust. So we have tried to combine description with analysis of current controversies, indicating the directions in which the system is likely to go. And in so far as we care about educational provision for our own nation's children, we seek, finally, not only to understand the Soviet Union better, but to discover whether there are areas in which we can learn from it to enrich ourselves and our children.

In undertaking this investigation, we soon realised how little has been written in the West about Soviet special education. Apart from John Dunstan's book on the gifted, the literature on Soviet education contains scant reference to the gifted and handicapped, and nothing that combines the two. Ours is the first work to do so. It is a challenging and worthwhile field of research not only because much ignorance exists in the West about Soviet special education, but because, at least in terms of the gifted, the USSR has patently achieved success in identifying and nurturing talent in a whole range of spheres of excellence. Yet it is provision for the physically and mentally handicapped that may ultimately offer the greatest reward in terms of shared experience. It is evident from the recent discovery of the pioneering work being done in conductive education in Hungary that Western specialists do have something to learn from their colleagues in Eastern Europe. Significantly, two of the contributors to this book, Andrew Sutton and Mike Lambert, are themselves pioneers in applying East European methods for the benefit of children in Britain. Since we are talking of children who need help more than all others, it is vital that we seek to discover what our Soviet colleagues are doing. This is precisely what Andrew Sutton generally, Avril Suddaby with slow learners and Mike Lambert with the blind-deaf have sought to do. As Mike Lambert puts it,

> If glasnost makes access by Westerners to Soviet defectological expertise easier, one hopes that interested professionals will not be slow in examining and applying it - for the benefit of the deaf-blind everywhere.

No understanding of deviations from the norm is possible without knowledge of the norm. Before some contributors examine aspects of special education, therefore, James Muckle presents a picture of the educational experience of the Soviet young person; not the exceptional or disadvantaged, but the overall majority (some 85% of the school-age population). He also reminds us how often we unconsciously regard our own system and values as being 'natural' and those of others as 'unnatural'. This underlines the book's objective in explaining the underlying attitudes and values of educators, parents and children in the Soviet Union, and attempting to relate Soviet experience to the needs and philosophy of that society, as well as those in the West. What do they do that is different from us? And why? What can we learn from one another?

In regard to special education for the gifted, the Soviet Union would seem to have demonstrated that the highest realisation of human potential can be most effectively achieved through the planned application of society's resources; it has attained this goal in a range of fields of excellence and its achievements have been inspired by the notion that talent can and should be identified early and nurtured both for the benefit of individual self-fulfilment and for the enjoyment and pride that the community gains from the application of that talent. This appears to be so not simply in musicianship, ballet, art and mathematics, but in sport as well. There is clearly a strong belief that the culture of the body is as vital as that of the mind for the harmonious development of the individual and, ultimately, for the health of society. This belief in the parity of mental and physical culture in human development provides a conviction that talent in physical culture should be treated no differently from talent in mental culture. In other words, a budding gymnast should be given as much opportunity to develop his or her gifts as are promising ballet dancers. This contrasts with the conventional Western approach in leaving talent development to the physical, moral and financial resources of the individual, and the stigma attached to the cultivation of sports excellence on a par with, say, music and ballet. All the same, as Dunstan, Riordan and especially Avis show, the spirit of glasnost is producing a number of modifications to the system, particularly as a result of pressure from the recipients of the special education - the students themselves.

If there were one distinguishing feature of the Soviet system of special education that is worth highlighting, it is the notion that 'a child is not what it is, but what society makes it.' What the contributors here all emphasise is that in order to understand the child we must first understand the society. The rewards, after all, can be handsome, especially to the children who need them most.

NOTE

1. M. Gorbachov, Report on the 70th Anniversary of the October Revolution, Soviet Weekly, 7 November 1987, p. x.

Chapter One

THE EDUCATIONAL EXPERIENCE OF THE SOVIET YOUNG PERSON

James Muckle

INTRODUCTION

In March 1987 the deputy headmistress of an English primary school was discussing early childhood education with the manageress of a Soviet kindergarten (for children aged 3 to 6 or 7). The Englishwoman, who had a particular interest in infant education (age 5 to 7), remarked afterwards, 'It was amazing that two people with so much in common professionally in almost every respect should in some ways be separated by such a gulf. On some fundamental matters we were a hundred miles apart.'

This remark highlights a major task of the student of comparative education: to appreciate and remain conscious of those points at which his or her own experience of schooling, cultural assumptions and intellectual background do not correspond with those of the nation whose education is being studied. The 'fundamental matters' about which the interlocutors disagreed in the encounter referred to concerned the apparently conflicting rights and roles of parents and public institutions in the upbringing of children: the duty of a mother who has trained professionally to serve society in a professional role and her duty to raise her children. These issues, however, are by no means uncontroversial within either Soviet or British society. One simply cannot say, in this as in other matters, 'The Soviets take the view ...' and 'The British believe ...'. Attitudes to such matters change as a nation's way of life changes; nevertheless, it is possible to make some generalisations as to the predominant current view in a society.

The student of other educational systems, however able

and sensitive he or she may be, often takes some time to appreciate such basic differences in attitude. Ideas of what is 'natural' or self-evident are not easily changed. Students and schoolchildren in different cultures do not necessarily even learn in the same ways: some are taught to accept the teacher and the textbook as unchallengeable authorities, while others are encouraged to question and criticise. Some can learn well only from lectures and books, while others are skilled at picking up non-verbal signals. Values and aims differ fundamentally, as does the classroom ethic. The very concepts of 'school' and 'lesson' differ across cultures. For all these reasons, the outline of the Soviet education system which follows will be worthless if it consists of no more than an account of the organisation and administration of schooling in the USSR, a list of the subjects children study and the ages at which they enter school and change course. This chapter will attempt, in addition, to explain the underlying attitudes of educators, parents and children. Authors of following chapters will inevitably make this point again and again. We are nevertheless inevitably in a 'double-bind' here, for the reader of whatever nationality must remember that this first chapter is an Englishman's attempt at elucidating the Soviet system; whatever objectivity it has is achieved within this unavoidable limitation.

The theme of this book is the education of the child and young person who is in some way exceptional or disadvantaged. The purpose of this chapter is to describe the education and upbringing received by the majority of Soviet children, 'normal', average, ordinary, or whatever term is preferred. The position of the others is intended to emerge in clearer relief by contrast. At the time of writing the Soviet education system is changing. In 1984 it was announced that certain reforms were to be instituted; a discussion document appeared and comments were invited. Partly in the light of the public discussion which followed, a revised version of the document, known in its official English translation as 'Guidelines for Reform of General and Vocational Schools', (1) was issued with the full authority of the Central Committee of the Communist Party of the Soviet Union. The major administrative measures included are all dealt with later in this chapter or in other parts of this book. They include the starting of compulsory education one year earlier than previously, at six, the changes in vocational education both in the general-education school and in terms of the arrangements at age 15, and how to foster talent in schoolchildren. Because these changes are being implemented at the moment, readers of this book will understand that, for example, although eleven years of compulsory education is now the norm, the mass of Soviet children will not have completed that period until 1997, and the educational background of the vast majority of Soviet adults will remain ten-year education (or even eight for older, and seven for the elderly) for many years to come. Similarly, the numbering of classes in Soviet schools will be in a state of confusion until the reform has gone through the system, and this will be reflected in the writing of this chapter.

THE PRE-SCHOOL YEARS

Many Soviet children are entered in an institution from a very early age. The creche (<u>yasli</u>), overseen by the Ministry of Health and often organised by the mother's workplace, takes them from the age of three months, and the kindergarten, (<u>detsky sad</u>), from three; often enough these days the institution is known as a <u>yasli-sad</u> and caters for the whole age range from three months to six or seven years. Kindergartens and the joint institutions are under the control of the Ministry of Education of the Republic concerned. Education is not compulsory until the age of six, so the first decision the parents have to make is whether to send the child to a pre-school establishment. The decision is not a wholly straightforward matter.

For several reasons the parents may have little choice. The state needs the labour of women - unemployment problems have not struck the Soviet Union on anything approaching the Western European scale yet - and 92% of women of working age are in employment. (2) Salaries for both men and women are not high (again, reckoned by Western standards, though comparison is difficult for many reasons) and most couples need two incomes. Soviet homes are not equipped with so many labour-saving devices as in other highly developed countries, shopping is stressful and very time-consuming; despite ideological belief in the equality of the sexes, many Soviet men expect their womenfolk to do all the housework and shopping. The flats in which people live in cities are relatively small (eight to ten square metres allowed per capita, depending on the city concerned). (3) Consequently, in Russia and the Northern

3

Republics in the early 1980s, 56% of families had only one child; a mere 6% had three or more, though more recently the situation has been changing. (4) (In the Central Asian Republics, where traditional attitudes attach great prestige to the ability to procreate and to having large families, the situation has always been quite different.) In coping with daily routines it is essential for parents to have their children, or more likely child, looked after by others. That means, for the majority in the Russian Republic at least, the creche and kindergarten.

However, there are alternatives. The traditional upbringer of children in Russia is their grandmother, and until a few years ago she was regarded by many young parents as a desirable alternative. But nowadays many Soviet grandmothers are refusing to carry out their traditional role; (5) as more kindergarten places become available, the babushki see no reason why they should accept the commitment. Children are, however, sometimes minded by friends or relations. Parents from the professional and intellectual classes, who can arrange to work at home for some of the time - which is scarcely a large proportion of the population - may manage to look after children themselves. Parents may pay to have their children minded, or, of course, one parent, almost invariably the mother, can choose to take a break from working life in order to bring up the children, though many fear that career prospects may be severely damaged by this course of action.

The official attitude to pre-school education, represented by the kindergarten manageress in the incident with which this chapter began, has tended to be that establishments with well-trained, caring staff are unquestionably the best place for young children to be during the day. They receive expert care, and, most important for a young member of a socialist society, they develop social relationships with their peers which are as significant as emotional relationships with their parents. Furthermore, the argument goes, even if they spend relatively little time with their parents, there is every likelihood that the quality of their relationship with mother and father will be enhanced, and the quality is what is important. But if all this is so, why should parents seek an alternative to pre-school establishments?

They may do so simply because a place for their child is not available: the problem is more acute with the younger age group, as creche places are much less easily available than those in kindergartens. (6) Half the total age group in fact attends a pre-school establishment, (7) but in some large Russian towns this proportion can reach 90% or even more; nevertheless, figures published in 1986-87 revealed that one and a half million more applications for pre-school places were received than could be satisfied. (8) And despite the attitude referred to previously - that pre-school is actually a better place to be than home - and despite also the feeling that a mother owes the duty of labour to the state, there are many Soviet parents who do not wish to be deprived of the experience of bringing up their own children. Recent legislation, making more generous arrangements for maternity leave and payment, has proved very popular indeed, and many mothers are taking maximum advantage of it. Women now have a right to partly-paid leave for one year after the birth of a child and 18 months' unpaid leave. More than half of all mothers are now taking one and a half years' leave, which is eight times more than previously; moreover the birth rate among urban women rose after these new arrangements were introduced. (9) There are even a few parents who feel strongly that <u>they</u> wish to take responsibility for imparting values to their child, even going so far as to express it in terms of 'putting off the brain-washing as long as possible'. Needless to say, this view would be indignantly rejected by very many Soviet educators. Nevertheless, an article in <u>Pravda</u> for 20 March 1987 concluded that it was a 'mistake' to have ever imagined that state upbringing of children was better than that given by the family. 'The foundation for physical and mental health is laid in the family and nowhere else.' (10)

There are many excellent kindergartens in the Soviet Union. This description of one of them serves to give the flavour of the whole class of institution. It is in an industrial suburb of a large city in Belorussia, and is attended by 380 children looked after by up to 28 <u>vospitateli</u>, nursery nurses in English terms, and most of the children's parents work in a car factory. (The words 'teacher' and 'headmistress' are not used in connection with kindergartens, since Soviet terminology distinguishes carefully those qualified to teach in schools from pre-school staff.) The manageress knows of only four families in the catchment area whose children do not attend. The kindergarten is open about twelve hours a day - there are some which operate twenty-four hours, a boarding system, in fact. The facilities include a gym, adventure playground and outside play area, a small swimming pool and a solarium, most of which were provided by local firms or enterprises on a self-help basis. The principal concern of the establishment is the general and moral development of the children and care for their physical well-being rather than formal instruction - though quite a lot of this obviously goes on. Music, art, poetry (in both Russian and Belorussian) and dance are all stressed; the children engage in performance arts with great relish. Meals are provided four times during this long day. Medical advice is readily available. Parents pay fees on a sliding scale from 20 rubles a month to nothing.

What is it like inside such an institution? Are children happy to go there? The point is made by sociologists that Soviet children are used to much closer contact with parents, other relations, neighbours and friends than is customary in Western Europe or America, that they are taught to regard all friendly adults as 'uncle' and 'aunt', and that they are consequently not unwilling to be handed over by their parents to others for many hours a day. (11) The almost total feminisation of this environment is regarded as something of a problem as it is even in secondary schools, where women teachers predominate. As to the running of the kindergartens, visitors often comment favourably on the quiet atmosphere and the orderliness in comparison with nurseries or infants' schools elsewhere. The purposeful activity is also favourably noted, but it is thought to be very highly teacher-directed rather than child-centred. In accord with the principles of Soviet morality, which will be discussed in more detail below, great emphasis is placed on collective work and play. The elementary labour training, which includes teaching children to keep clean, look after themselves and be independent, has its practical counterpart in other countries (though we shall discuss its ideological foundation later), but the understanding of 'independence' differs. In the USSR it appears to refer to the ability to look after oneself, tie shoelaces, wash hands and so on; the Western teacher would wish it to mean also sometimes even the child deciding for itself what it might do next - and how it might do it. Nevertheless, it must be said that Soviet pre-school children, by the end of their time in kindergarten, show a self-confidence and competence in dealing with visitors - strangers - which is clearly the result of training. (12)

COMPULSORY EDUCATION

Six-year-olds in school

One of the principal and almost certainly the most controversial of the measures introduced by the 1984 reform of the school system was the introduction of universal compulsory education from the age of six. No matter that many Soviet children in certain Republics had been in school at six for several years and that an earlier start is common in almost every other European country except Sweden, the change from seven to six was quite vociferously opposed by a substantial minority of parents and educationists. Remarks were heard like 'Childhood is being cut short' or 'School is no place for six-year-olds'. (13) This is all the more strange in view of the high proportion of Soviet children who attend pre-school establishments for many long hours a day as it is. Why is school regarded as 'no place' for them?

To answer this question we need to understand the whole concept of 'school' as it is perceived in the Soviet Union. The tradition in the Russian Empire, which in this respect as in some others survives to this day - but which is now beginning to change, was of an extremely formal classroom atmosphere with much rote-learning and a very high factual content, almost entirely teacher-centred and making scant concession to the immature stage of development of the child. The work of Froebel was known in Russia in the 1870s: there was indeed a St Petersburg Froebelian Society which produced a journal called The Kindergarten, but such notions of early childhood education were too foreign to Russian practice to gain much currency. (14) After the 1917 Revolution, in the 1920s, Russian schools experimented with methods based on the ideas of such as John Dewey and Helen Parkhurst, but - possibly again because these notions were simply too new and surprising in the Russian context - there was a return to traditional methods under Stalin. (15) There is, in fact, an objection to informal methods which is almost ideological: the authority of the teacher must not be called into question, and the curriculum, which has been arrived at by the processes of 'scientific socialism', must be conveyed 'systematically'. (16) Despite the possible attraction of methods which might involve children working cooperatively in groups (which could just as well be termed 'collectives', giving them political respectability), until very recently the reception classes of Soviet schools taught seven-year-olds by very formal, though not, of course, necessarily ineffective, and overtly didactic methods. Everyone, parents and teachers alike, knows such methods to be totally inappropriate for teaching infants, which explains why they think 'school is no place for six-year-olds'. The introduction of compulsory schooling for children at the younger age has had to be accompanied by measures to sweeten the pill: the option of holding the first-year classes in kindergartens and the promise of much more appropriate treatment, premises and equipment for the reception classes in regular schools. In the year 1986-87 nearly a third of six-year-olds were taught in classes organised in kindergartens. (17) We shall return to the subject of teaching methods in due course.

THE GENERAL EDUCATION SCHOOL

Organisation and admission

Since 1986, Soviet parents have been entering their children at six for primary education, with the expectation that they will stay in compulsory full-time schooling for eleven years. In rural areas the school entered may be a four-year primary or a nine-year 'incomplete secondary' institution, but for the most part it will be an all-age, unstreamed, comprehensive, co-educational, primary-with-secondary school serving a catchment area, and with a curriculum nationally decided which is taught using textbooks officially prescribed. There are about 140,000 such schools in the USSR. (18)

Nevertheless, some latitude is possible. There exist 'schools with special profiles', to which parents from outside the normal catchment area may send their children, if they can get a place. These schools often have great prestige, and the question of admissions to them (and the almost unlimited scope for corruption, 'connections' and influence in placing children in them) has recently been the subject of much heated debate in the Soviet press. (19) A later chapter (by Dunstan) in this book deals with the whole issue. One Moscow headmistress of a special mathematics school declared with pride in 1984: 'One mother sat outside my office for three days at the beginning of term until I agreed to admit her son.' It must be gratifying for staff to teach in so popular an institution.

Underlying spirit and aims

A fundamental principle of the Soviet school is what is termed the 'unity of instruction and upbringing'; in other words, the ethical and moral aims of education are no less important than the academic and scientific. This most important fact profoundly affects the experience that any Soviet child undergoes in school, and the nature of the morality conveyed accounts for the distinctive flavour of the education system. (20)

The aim of Soviet education, as any pedagogue there will confirm, is to create a 'new type of person', who has certain moral attributes and ideological attitudes. These are Soviet patriotism, which is not meant to be mindless jingoism, but love for the first country in the world to embrace socialism and to create a workers' state; proletarian internationalism - support for the workers of the world in their struggle for liberation from capitalist exploiters and respect for their culture and tradition; socio-political awareness, involving strong communist convictions and a dialectical-materialist attitude; militant atheism; respect for labour and the skills of the craftsman, the desire to participate in socially useful work and the determination to learn the skills to be able to do so; a collectivist attitude and avoidance of egotistic individualism; strong ethical-moral principles, respect for the law and the duties of a citizen; acceptance of the responsibility of bringing up the next and future generations in the spirit of communism; a conservationist attitude to natural resources, natural beauty, the environment, historical monuments and the achievements of culture. A Soviet citizen is expected, moreover, through his or her education to extend knowledge and mental horizons, to improve aesthetic awareness and to keep physically fit. This embraces every aspect of an all-round personality as perceived by Soviet orthodoxy. The overall aim of the system is often neatly summarised as the creation of 'a well-trained work-force of broad general culture'.

The ethical and moral upbringing aims are striven for both in class and outside. The youth organisations to which a large majority of children belong, the Octobrists (to age 8), the Young Pioneers (to 15) and the Communist League of Youth after 15 (to 28), play a large part. Extra-curricular activities and clubs contribute too. Certain subjects in the curriculum are designed specifically to contribute to the instilling of these attitudes. Last, but not least, the teaching of every subject in the programme of study has to emphasise these values through the knowledge it conveys, the passages set for reading, the questions given for discussion and the interpretation of the facts presented. There is no secret about this; a vast literature exists instructing teachers how to do it.

A particularly significant subject in the school curriculum is Labour Training. (21) Its position is very much more than a matter of practical training: it has considerable philosophical importance and is firmly believed to be of great moral significance for the child, which is why discussion of it is included here under the heading of the 'underlying spirit' of the system. Marxist-Leninist thought has always attached importance to labour, especially industrial manual work, and the economic wealth which the worker creates by the sweat of his brow. To be a member of the working class, more especially the industrial proletariat, carries prestige - or is intended to. Respect for the skills of the craftsman, knowledge of industrial and agricultural processes and production and understanding of the social and economic importance of all this are known, following a phrase of Karl Marx, as 'polytechnical education' and are seen as vital elements in a communist upbringing. In recent years the Soviet school has tried to adopt a more rational and consistent approach to this ideal, but the system has been bedevilled over the years by the need to train workers for the economy and the sheer difficulties of organising effective labour training at school. Even since the most recent reform, strident complaints have been reaching the press about ineffective teaching and inadequate facilities for labour instruction. (22)

Nevertheless, the intention is clear: labour appears on the timetable for the whole of a child's school career, and as we have seen, is even present in the kindergarten. Up to the age of 12 the Soviet child receives labour education which ranges from performing odd jobs about the home, school and garden, to an understanding of a range of general trade skills, together with some theoretical information about the contribution of various types of work to the economy. In most ways this instruction resembles the workshop crafts and home economics which are taught in Western schools. However, in the USSR notions of allowing boys to learn cookery and girls metalwork are regarded with near derision; 'equal opportunities' on this level are not taken seriously. In the new year 8 (age 13) pupils begin to specialise in a general trade area, and in year 10 they select a specific industrial or agricultural specialism; when they leave school at the end of year 11 they should, if all has gone well, receive a certificate qualifying them to seek a job in a factory, firm, enterprise or on a farm at full salary the day after they leave school. Thus is it intended to achieve more than one aim: to improve attitudes to labour and discourage children from any distaste at getting their hands dirty, to teach them about industry and the world of work, and to provide workers for the economy without the need for a training period after school is finished. Whatever the practical effects of this policy, and whatever complaints about its inadequacies appear in the press, the important thing to remember is that labour instruction forms a significant part of the education of every Soviet child, and that its share of the teaching time has increased significantly over the last ten to fifteen years.

School buildings

The qualities valued by an educational establishment are inevitably reflected in the appearance of the buildings it occupies. The pupil entering a Soviet school is probably going into a building in a city which looks very like the flats which surround it; extensive playing fields and obvious sports facilities are not a feature. The city school is often quite difficult for the visitor to find, and even local people are not always sure which school is which. This may be because the schools by long Russian tradition have numbers, rather than names - a fact which reinforces the notion that 'all schools are the same'. Inside the building quotations from the sayings of any prominent person from Leonardo da Vinci to Lenin, slogans, state symbols and coats of arms are prominent. Portraits or busts of Lenin are everywhere, but the present leadership is much less often represented than in the past. The importance of academic prowess is underlined by the gallery of photographs of <u>otlichniki</u>, the pupils consistently receiving excellent marks. In one school visited in Minsk these amounted to 100 from a roll of 1,300. Children's work is displayed on the walls, but very much less widely than in England. (Pupils tend to produce albums rather than wall-mounted projects.) Classroom displays are usually very professionally produced by the teachers, and the same themes ('USSR - Our Homeland', 'Lenin in London' in the English room) appear all over the country. Classrooms have an obvious standard arrangement: rows of desks, bookshelves, displays, notice-boards with lists of duties, audio-visual equipment, storage space for necessary materials, and ubiquitous pot plants. Notice-boards in the public areas of the school often carry the rules, rights and privileges of both parents and pupils, the aims of the institution and the plans of the staff for the immediate future.

The primary years

The Soviet pupil arrives at school for the first time, perhaps passing through decorated streets and after hearing festive messages on radio and television, on 1 September (the 'Day of Knowledge'), carrying flowers for the teacher. A short ceremony, usually held partly on the steps outside the school and attended by all the children old and new, parents and other members of the public who wish to show their interest in education, will include a speech from the head teacher reminding all present of their duty as citizens or future citizens and of the concern of the Party for the rising generation. Children may contribute poems and little speeches, the youth organisations will be prominently represented, images of Lenin will be on display (flowers are often laid in tribute), music may be played, flags raised and national anthems played or sung. The first school bell will be ceremonially rung and older pupils take younger ones by the hand and lead them into their classrooms. (23) The very first lesson in recent years has been a 'peace lesson', recalling the horrors of war and the need for world peace in speeches, poetry and song. (24) These rituals admirably reflect the values of the state and the importance attached to education, and they must serve to make a child's first day at school a memorable and significant occasion.

We have already mentioned the fact that many children may actually experience their first compulsory school year in a kindergarten rather than a school, but even so the instruction given there will be the responsibility of the local general-education school. In the first year at least the atmosphere and teaching methods will be less stiff than implied by the misgivings felt by opponents of school at six; for the remaining three years of primary education children will receive formal instruction in their native language and/or Russian, arithmetic, music, art, labour and PE, along with one lesson a week in the first two years entitled 'Acquaintance with the world around' (elementary geography, science and general social awareness) and in the last two a lesson of nature study. For most of this time the children will be taught by their class teacher; there are 20 weekly lessons in year 1, rising to 25 in year 4. (25) A lesson traditionally lasts 45 minutes, though it is shorter in class 1. The school day begins between 8 and 8.30; there are breaks between lessons, in some of which teachers organise movement games for the younger pupils and allow and encourage older ones to do extra physical education. School operates Monday to Saturday, and lessons finish by early afternoon. Where school buildings are not adequate to house all children of school age, a second shift operates, which is in effect a second school meeting in the afternoon. Such groups tend now to be small if they exist, as the practice can scarcely be regarded as satisfactory.

The 'extended day'

It might seem, then, that Soviet children spend a rather short time every day in school. All the same, with 92% of mothers at work, very many families are clearly unable to receive their child at midday when lessons finish. The system allows for this in various ways. A midday meal may be provided at minimal cost in the school canteen. The Young Pioneer organisation has Pioneer houses or even 'palaces' which open in the afternoons and provide facilities for hobbies, arts, crafts, music, dancing and many other sporting, cultural and what might be termed creative recreational activities. There are schools for children to learn to play musical instruments and in some places centres for those talented in art. Many schools, the figure is given as 86,400, (26) organise an 'extended day', by which pupils are looked after until their parents collect them or they can return home and be sure of being admitted. Homework is supervised (and homework is set after every lesson in all subjects), remedial work is conducted for those who have dropped behind, and clubs meet. Though sometimes complaints are heard that arrangements for the extended day are unsatisfactory, it is noticeable that, in theory at least, Soviet educators are interested only in organising

13

Table 1.1 Model Curriculum for the Secondary General School
Periods per week per form

	I	II	III	IV	V	VI	VII	VIII	IX	X	XI	Total
First language and literature	7	9	11	11	11	9	6	5	5	3	3	80
Mathematics	4	6	6	6	6	6	6	6	6	4/5	4	60.5
Principles of Information Science and Computer Technology	—	—	—	—	—	—	—	—	—	1	2	3
History	—	—	—	—	2	2	2	2	3	4	3	18
Principles of Soviet State and Law	—	—	—	—	—	—	—	—	1	—	—	1
Social Studies	—	—	—	—	—	—	—	—	—	0/2	2/1	2.5
Ethics and Psychology of Family Life	—	—	—	—	—	—	—	—	0/1	1/0	—	1
The World Around Us	1	1	—	—	—	—	—	—	—	—	—	2
Nature Study	—	—	1	1	1	—	—	—	—	—	—	3
Geography	—	—	—	—	—	2	3	2	2	2/1	—	10.5
Biology	—	—	—	—	—	2	2	2	2	1	1/2	10.5
Physics	—	—	—	—	—	—	2	2	3	4/3	4	14.5
Astronomy	—	—	—	—	—	—	—	—	—	—	1	1
Chemistry	—	—	—	—	—	—	—	3	3/2	2	2	9.5
Technical Drawing	—	—	—	—	—	—	1	1	—	—	—	2
Foreign Language	—	—	—	—	4	3	2	2	1	1	1	14
Art	2	1	1	1	1	1	1	—	—	—	—	8
Music and Singing	2	1	1	1	1	1	1	—	—	—	—	8
Physical Education	2	2	2	2	2	2	2	2	2	2	2	22
Elementary Military Training	—	—	—	—	—	—	—	—	—	2	2	4
Labour and Vocational Training (1)	2	2	2	2	2	2	2	3	3	4	4	28
TOTAL	20	22	24	24	30	30	30	30	31	31	31	303
Socially-useful Productive Labour (Compulsory)(2)	—	1	1	1	2	2	2	3	3	4	4	23
Options	—	—	—	—	—	2	2	2	2	4	4	14
Labour Practice (in days) (3)	—	—	—	—	10	10	10	16	16	20	—	—

Notes
1. Vocational training takes place in forms VII–XI. One period a week in each of these forms is devoted to the course 'Principles of Production. Choosing a Career'.
2. The time allocated to compulsory socially-useful productive labour may be concentrated.
3. 3 hours a day in forms V to VII, 4 in forms VIII to IX, 6 in form X.

Source
Byulleten' normativnykh aktov Ministerstva prosveshcheniya SSSR, 1985, no 6, p 24.

constructive activity for pupils, even in a recreational context. There is no feeling that it is part of the education service's responsibility to provide purely social activities for young people.

Secondary education to fifteen

At the age of ten the Soviet child moves on to the secondary phase of education when he or she enters class 5 (by the new numbering). For most children this means no change of building, but all subjects are now taught by specialists rather than by a class teacher.

It is easier to represent the curriculum followed in tabular form than to describe it in words (Table 1.1). On this chart numbers represent the weekly lessons in the subject concerned, and where two figures are given in one column, the first refers to the first half of the year and the second to the second half. As in primary education, this curriculum is arrived at by interpretation of criteria which include the requirements of the state, and the need to form all-round developed communist personalities. Knowledge is ordered according to the Marxist troika of man - nature - society, but is classified under traditional subject headings for purposes of being conveyed to schoolchildren. The dilemma of how to convey a unified system of knowledge while teaching fairly rigidly circumscribed subjects is resolved by looking for and stressing 'inter-subject links' in all syllabuses. (27)

It will be seen from the table that art and music teaching ends in class seven, while the sciences begin with biology in class 6 and expand in the senior years. The native language and literature, along with mathematics, continue to occupy a prominent position. Literature is, therefore, the only subject in the aesthetic 'cycle' which is taught throughout secondary education. History is introduced and slowly increases its share of the timetable; it is joined later by related subject areas such as Soviet state and law (and social studies, for which it is seen as a preparation, after age 15). Geography is taught from age 11; physical education continues throughout, as does labour training, which is supplemented for two years by its related subject technical drawing. One foreign language, English for about half of Soviet children, otherwise German, French, less often Spanish or in a very few other cases some other language, appears in year five but by class 9 finds its period allocation so diminished that it looks almost like a waste of time.

The content of the syllabuses of some of these subjects and the methods by which they are taught have been the subject of heated controversy for some years. Many Soviet educators have an almost ineradicable notion that education concerns the presentation of facts - many, many facts; and this has led to children being stuffed to bursting with an enormous amount of information. The only way this could be mastered, if at all, was by rote, and the average and less able child could scarcely be expected to master all the concepts required. A major requirement of the new syllabuses compiled in the light of the 1984 reforms is to reduce the overloading by stripping away superfluous and repetitive material, and by increasing the conceptual as opposed to the factual content. (28)

In mathematics, while the syllabuses still seem very full, the content has in fact been considerably reduced. It is in this subject that Soviet teachers most often discuss problems of remedial teaching and of the difficulties of keeping a mixed-ability class together. ('Mixed-ability' is not used in Soviet terminology, since psychologists have always given much less credence there to differences in 'intelligence'; they prefer to speak of differences in achievement.) Russian as a native language is taught very formally, with traditional grammar, syntax, punctuation, phonetics, morphology and so on, in the belief that accurate and literate communicative abilities will result - but in fact they do not. It is interesting that the Soviet educationist's response to this fact is not to call for formal linguistic instruction to be scrapped, but to express determination to improve methods of teaching based on the same assumption that study of grammar will improve the ability to communicate. 'Creative writing' is practised much less often in the USSR than in Britain - at least in class; out-of-school clubs are another matter. Soviet children have to read a very wide range of literature during their school career: wide both in quantity and quality. At best this is taught imaginatively and broadens the children's horizons while bringing them face to face with aesthetic experience; all too often it is stultifying cramming with stereotyped ready-made interpretations, concentrating almost exclusively on the social, political and historical significance of the works studied.

Scientific education, along with all other subjects in the curriculum, sets out to give children a Marxist-Leninist and dialectical-materialist world-view. In the sciences, materialism and resistance to religious views of the world are prominent. Biology teaching is centred around Darwin and evolution, but it is still being said that this very difficult concept is not satisfactorily imparted to children yet. Soviet science teachers seek to increase the amount of time devoted to experimental work in class; at present much of it is performed as demonstrations by the teacher, and it is not clear that the profession is ready yet to encourage a great expansion of independent pupil activity in the laboratory. The practical, industrial and ecological implications of scientific subjects are stressed; the human side - famous scientists and technologists, Russian, Soviet and foreign, and their activity - is used to inculcate patriotism and proletarian internationalism.

History is regarded as a most important subject ideologically, and great attention is paid to conveying 'correct' political orthodoxy in the interpretation of historical events. The syllabus covers very many areas of the world, devoting slightly more time to 'general' as opposed to Soviet history. The same could be said about geography, recent syllabuses for which show a refreshingly enlightened attitude to other nations and other cultures. However, field work is much less highly developed than in the West and the bulk of the time is devoted to classroom instruction.

It is in the arts, music especially, that some of the most encouraging and adventurous work has been done in recent years, but this has not been without controversy and campaigning on both sides. Music lessons have been transformed from dull singing exercises and boring talks on composers' lives into lively occasions in which intelligent musical perception, emotional response, vocal and instrumental performance, and to some small extent compositional activities have improved pupil attitudes and teacher morale considerably. (29) Something of the same is happening in art: much more creative work in several different media and much less drawing of 'two apples on a plate'.

Foreign language teachers concentrate on oral skills in the earlier years, but are forced in view of the single lesson per week in year 9 to cut their losses and try to develop reading and comprehension ability only. Nevertheless, standards of achievement are far from negligible, and this is partly due to quite high motivation on the part of many pupils and the fact that syllabuses are carefully defined as regards their content of foreign words and structures to be mastered and the topics which pupils are to be able to talk about in the foreign language. (30)

In class 9 two subjects appear which fall into the category of civic and family education. Principles of Soviet state and law aims to acquaint pupils with their rights and duties as future citizens, to inform them about the law as it affects them (in an attempt to reduce juvenile delinquency, which is regarded partly as a consequence of ignorance of the law), and to reinforce political and ideological education. Ethics and psychology of family life is an attempt to come to grips with the appalling divorce rate (9.8 million marriages in 1985 and 3.4 million divorces) (31) and to give young people some conception of the nature of marriage, child-raising and human relationships as it affects them personally and in relation to the rest of society. This course contains no sex education (which is held to have been dealt with in about four lessons of human biology in class 9) and in fact deprecates the importance of sexual relationships. It has been criticised for this, and various experiments in family education continue.

Examinations

With the exception of two lessons per week of optional courses this is the curriculum undergone by every child in the mass general-education schools, and for 95% of their time by children in schools with special profiles too. Not only the subjects and the number of lessons, but the detailed content of the syllabuses and the textbooks used (and to a very large extent also the teaching methods approved), are determined by central authority. Democracy and equality in the Soviet Union are taken to imply that everyone must experience the same content in their education. But how is mastery of that content assessed?

The Russian tradition in examinations at any level of the educational system is not one of written, but of oral testing. Questions are written or printed on slips of paper known as 'tickets', which lie face down on a table as in some conjuring trick and which are selected at random by the candidates. Pupils and students may be given some time to prepare and make notes, and then must stand before the examiners and give their answers orally. The main exceptions to this are Russian essay-writing and mathematics. Answers are marked on a scale with 5 as the 'excellent' mark, 4 as 'good' and 3 'satisfactory'; to receive 2 ('unsatisfactory') is a disgrace. The whole school population is judged on this scale, and to a large extent using the same examination questions, so it will be clear that there is little place for fine distinctions.

Recent (1987) moves have sought to extend the examining system to much younger children than at present - even in the primary school. (32) This is meeting ferocious opposition from those who see examinations as extremely stressful occasions which should be inflicted on older teenagers only. Moreover, it is intended to introduce more written examinations, which will be an even greater break with tradition.

Informal assessment of children takes place in all classes and promotion to the next class depends to some extent on success in these tests, criteria for which are laid down and published in the subject syllabuses. But the major hurdle is encountered as children approach the age of fifteen, at the end of the new class 9. (33) Children take only Russian (oral and a written composition) and mathematics (also one oral and one written examination). A further feature of all Soviet public examinations which is often overlooked is that the examination questions are published several months before the examination data, sold publicly, and used by teachers and pupils in classroom rehearsals and revision work. (34) The effect of this is less at age 15, since the exact mathematical examples to be used are not specified, only the type of question. But huge lists of actual essay titles appear, and the pupil will know that, if he picks up oral geometry 'ticket' number 16 from the table he will have to prove Pythagoras's theorem, and so on. At a later stage, the fact that exact questions in such subjects as literature, history and social studies are known inevitably leads to the rote learning of acceptable answers. The fact is recognised and deplored by the better Soviet teachers, as press correspondence amply demonstrates. And finally, the whole examination is run and administered within and by the staff of the child's school, who naturally have an interest in his or her success. A visit at examination time from an external moderator in the shape of a representative of the local education office is regarded as a misfortune. However, if there were to be any dispute about the fairness of the conduct of the examination, a largely oral and school-based system lacking in systematic checking is not liable to much adjustment. In fact, any complaint from outside agencies usually comes from the higher education establishments which say that schools are sometimes absurdly generous in their marking.

What happens at age 15

Until a few years ago full-time formal schooling ended at this age for many children, and the eight-year course, as it then was, was known as 'incomplete' secondary education. As more resources for education became available the compulsory period was extended to ten years, but it was not until 1975 that the authorities were able to announce with confidence that every child starting school in that year would certainly complete ten years. Now, since 1986, eleven-year compulsory education is promised for all. Full-time education for the entire age group 15-17 is therefore a fairly recent innovation. What considerations has it brought in its wake?

Reading between the lines of the Soviet press, it seems clear that these years used to be seen by teachers as a finishing school for the rather more able pupil. It was at one time assumed that the others would take themselves off, if they decided to continue their full-time education, to another establishment, such as a vocational school of one sort or another. Those who stayed in the general school were expected to get on with an academic education, and to do it pretty well - regularly to get marks of 4 and 5, in other words. For a pupil to be awarded a 3, despite its designation as 'satisfactory', was seen as something of an insult. When opportunities were extended, many more pupils chose to stay in the upper classes of the general schools, in the hope of gaining entry to higher education. Their expectations of employment in jobs carrying higher prestige were consequently raised. Meanwhile industry claimed to be experiencing a shortage of trained workers. The reforms of 1984 seek to remedy this situation. (35)

Before looking at the situation as it is developing, let us see what other types of establishment have hitherto been available at age 15. The first of these was the PTU or vocational-technical college, which accepted students without an entrance examination at 15 for a three-year course which partly continued general education but spent about 60% of the time on specialist trade training. The second main type was the secondary-specialist educational establishment, known as a tekhnikum or college (uchilishche), the former if the profile fell into the categories of industry, construction, transport, agriculture or economics, and the latter if it was educational, medical, musical, theatrical or the like. The training given in these establishments would be of an advanced level, short of that provided by universities or institutes of higher education, but of professional or semi-professional status. Thus they might train nurses and other health and leisure workers, kindergarten staff, agricultural technicians, toolmakers, and a variety of other workers. Until recently about 60% of the pupils at age 15 would continue in the general school, about 30% in the PTU and about 10% in secondary specialist education. This ratio varied considerably (in Leningrad very many more attended PTU), but in general it gives a reasonably accurate impression.

The intention is now to discourage all but the best-equipped from staying on at school and, if possible, to double entry to the PTUs. Industry is said to need the trained workers which these colleges can produce; higher education and society in general cannot cope with over-qualified people who will not take what they see as low-status jobs. To popularise the PTUs they have been reformed, so that soon all of them will give a full secondary education certificate as well as trade training, and in theory any qualified leaver with an 'excellent' certificate may apply for entry to university - so no absolutely irrevocable decision is taken when entering the college. They are now re-designated SPTUs, S for 'secondary', to indicate this new feature. Students are paid for the work they do and the goods they produce in the course of their training, which will probably prove something of an incentive to young people to train there. But the fact remains that the previous poor reputation of these colleges together with the attractions of the mainstream route from secondary to higher education will remain strong. Soviet educators speak of counselling and professional guidance of pupils at 14 and 15; but if the new proportions are to be realised, some selection by achievement or some compulsion will probably be necessary. Over such matters ambitious Soviet parents are not easily led by the nose.

21

Curriculum 15-17 and examinations

In the last two years of school the academic content of the syllabuses followed increases in seriousness. The Russian language course, where it is taught as native, is completed, and Russian lessons are devoted to literature. Mathematics is extended into calculus and the conceptually more difficult branches of the art; computer studies and information science has recently been introduced and is popular with pupils. Great attention is paid to the ideological benefits of history lessons, and social studies are added to this for further reinforcement of political orthodoxy. All three science subjects continue, physics lessons increase in number, and astronomy is added as a culmination of mathematical and physics education. Some elementary military training takes place as a preparation for military service for boys - but girls do it too. Labour and vocational training and the attendant obligation to perform socially useful labour occupy a good quarter of curriculum time. Optional courses account still for only a handful of weekly lessons, but they represent a slight opportunity to specialise in preparation, perhaps, for higher education.

The final leaving certificate examinations are more elaborate than those two years earlier. With the exception again of some mathematics and Russian, they are oral, and by the latest published regulations six subjects are taken: mathematics, history, sociology and literature are compulsory (as is Russian language if the candidate is a native speaker of another language, as nearly half the Soviet population is). For entry to higher education, four or five subjects are offered, of which Russian language and literature must be one; the others are to be related for the course which the applicant wishes to follow. For the most famous universities and institutes, entrance examinations are held (oral, as ever), and by reason of the timing of these exams, two chances are possible. Unsuccessful candidates may be given a document to show third or further choices of institution what they achieved in the entrance examinations for their first or second choice of institution.

The whole experience

It is impossible for the foreigner to know the exact nature of the experience of schooling in the Soviet Union as it must appear to the Soviet young person. Which of us can really know what our own school days gave us - at least until the traditional forty years on or until we have had the opportunity to compare them with something else, whatever that may be? Yet, as students of the Soviet Union and practitioners in the field of education, we must try to assess the nature of the Soviet educational experience if we seek to learn anything of benefit for our own practice or - more important, perhaps - if we wish to understand the Soviet Union. What could be more important for an insight into the Russian and Soviet mind than knowledge of the education every citizen receives? Let us try to make some generalisations.

Every Soviet child at age seven previously and six now, having very likely been in a pre-school establishment before that, enters a school in which society imparts a closely defined and detailed body of knowledge. It stresses the importance of the mastery of facts and is less concerned than it perhaps ought to be with discussion or argument. This is because it holds the conveying of a set system of values to be of paramount importance, and the values are often presented as facts. What the Americans call achievement-orientation, unshakeable belief in the absolutely essential nature of hard work and academic success, is prominent in the schools. The content which is conveyed is of a very serious and worthwhile nature. There are few easy options in Soviet education, and teachers are obliged to present the content to all pupils, however unwilling they may seem. At the same time, education is valued by society, partly for its own sake, partly because the presumed relationship between education and training and economic progress is recognised, and partly because through educational achievement young people can succeed in life. The most able products of the system intellectually are as critical of the world and aware as anywhere else, but the average school leaver may well not have realised that human knowledge in its present state is made up of uncertainties, fine distinctions and interesting dilemmas, rather than the easy definitions and doctrinaire judgements that their teachers have given them.

But are things set to change? The reforms set in motion in 1984 have been described as relatively conservative, and they are so as far as the more obvious features of organisation are concerned. However, closer inspection of moves within the schools, particularly as they concern teaching methods and the relationship between teachers and pupils, indicates that a radically new spirit is abroad. Is Soviet education at the end of the twentieth century beginning to suspect that its best interests are served by setting pupils free to discuss, argue, question, and by 'teaching them to think', as some Soviet educators would have it? 'We must get rid of authoritarian teaching,' they are saying; 'A teacher must be a friend and counsellor,' they assert. The present cry is for the 'pedagogics of cooperation' and for 'creative' workers and thinkers. Now it is undeniable that the will for change exists. At the time of writing the columns of <u>Uchitelskaya gazeta</u> (Teachers' Newspaper) are full of discussion and <u>real</u> outspoken discussion at last about the need to get away from old attitudes and old methods. Rank and file members of the profession seem unafraid to say what they really think of the show so far; ordinary, or fairly ordinary, journalists will say what they think of education ministers and their policies. To bring about any drastic change in attitudes that have become deeply ingrained over centuries of Russian tradition and decades of Soviet practice could not conceivably be done quickly. In other countries similar change has taken generations - if indeed it has happened at all. Leading Soviet educators speak of eight years as a minimum before newly trained young teachers could bring about any perceptible changes. Yet the enthusiasm and impatience of some young teachers are most noticeable. If the momentum of the 1984 reforms is not lost, and if the new spirit liberated by the 'Guidelines', the document which set the criteria for the changes, does not evaporate, what goes on in Soviet classrooms will be different in future.

The non-communist, non-Soviet observer may be tempted to make certain projections from this. The reforms call for creative thinking and an end to doctrinaire attitudes and stereotyped, ready-made opinions. Pupils are now to be taught to think for themselves. At the same time the reform 'Guidelines' call for correct political attitudes to be fostered. Educators brought up in the West European tradition would suppose that teaching methods which encourage children to explore ideas more freely instead of making them learn conclusions off by heart would lead inevitably in many cases to the pupils making up their own mind on political matters instead of adopting the views their teachers believed to be 'correct'. Soviet educationists argue rather differently. They do not deny the difficulty of persuading children of what they see as the truth; in fact pedagogical literature is full of exhortations to find ways of 'convincing' pupils. Nevertheless, they see no insoluble problem and no contradiction here. Marxism is 'scientific socialism' and is therefore demonstrably true; science will sooner or later find the answer to the difficulty of convincing children of the truth, and a methodology will be devised to take care of the problem. If Soviet leaders are right in this, future generations of young citizens will be more confident and committed to the ideals of their society than ever before. Even if that is so, the products of a system in which young people were taught to reason would be different from those of one which concentrates very largely on the mastery of factual content.

NOTES

1. The 'Guidelines' are published in USSR: New Frontiers of Social Progress. Documents of the first session of the USSR Supreme Soviet (eleventh convocation) April 11-12, 1984 (Progress, Moscow, 1984), pp. 50-78. For detailed accounts of the progress of the reform see J. Dunstan, 'Soviet education beyond 1984: a commentary on the reform guidelines,' Compare, vol. 15, no. 2 (1985), pp. 161-87, and B.B. Szekely, 'The new Soviet educational reform,' Comparative Education Review, vol. 30, no. 3 (1986), pp. 321-43.
2. Michael Binyon, Life in Russia (Hamilton, London, 1983), p.37.
3. J.H. Bater, The Soviet City (Edward Arnold, London, 1980), p. 106.
4. Binyon, p. 36.
5. N. Ward, 'Toddlers and working mothers: babushka or creche?' Britain-USSR, no. 51 (1977), pp. 9-12.
6. Binyon, p. 36.
7. Juergen Henze (ed.), Halbjahresbericht zur Bildungspolitik und Paedagogischen Entwicklung in der DDR, der UdSSR, der VR Polen, der CSSR und der VR China, 2. Halbjahr 1986 (Ruhr-Universität, Bochum, 1987), pp. 35-6 (quoting Izvestiya 18 and 20 November 1986). See also Basile Kerblay (translated by R. Swyer), Modern Soviet Society (Methuen, London, 1983).
8. Henze, p. 36.
9. 'The family', Current Digest of the Soviet Press,

vol. 39, no. 12 (1987), p.15.

10.   Ibid. p. 15.

11.   Kerblay, p. 153.

12.   For some of these insights into the care and education of infants I am indebted to a group of experienced British primary school teachers with whom I visited Soviet schools in 1987.

13.   Private information from Soviet educationists; continuous press coverage prior to the appearance of the 1984 confirmed Guidelines.

14.   On the Petersburg Froebelians, see F.A. Brokgauz and I.A. Efron, Entsiklopedichesky slovar (St Petersburg, 1890-1904), article 'Detsky sad', vol. 21, p. 353. On a typically hostile reaction of Russians to Froebelian ideas, see J. Muckle, 'Nikolai Leskov: educational journalist and imaginative writer', New Zealand Slavonic Journal, 1984, pp. 81-110, esp. pp. 88-9. For a recent Soviet view of Froebel, see M.F. Shabaeva, Istoriya pedagogiki (Prosveshchenie, Moscow, 1981), pp.56-62.

15.   A valuable contemporary account by an outsider of the system is Beatrice King, Changing Man (Gollancz, London, 1936), esp. pp. 21-4.

16.   See N.P. Kuzin et al. 'The development of pedagogical science,' Soviet Education vol. 25, no. 2 (1982), esp. p. 36.

17.   Henze, p. 36.

18.   L. Umansky, Soviet Living Standards Today and Tomorrow (Novosti, Moscow, 1986), p. 56.

19.   The controversy is admirably condensed in 'Special schools cater to elite's children,' Current Digest of the Soviet Press, vol. 39, no. 8 (1987), pp. 1-5, 14 and 20.

20.   Moral education is dealt with in numerous works; see, for example, George Avis (ed.), The Making of the Soviet Citizen (Croom Helm, London, 1987), J. Dunstan, 'Soviet moral education in theory and practice,' Journal of Moral Education, vol. 10, no. 3 (1981), pp. 192-202.

21.   This topic is dealt with in 'The School and the World of Work,' Chapter 4 of J. Muckle, A Guide to the Soviet Curriculum (Croom Helm, London, 1987).

22.   See, for example, 'The school reform makes slow progress,' Current Digest of the Soviet Press, vol. 38, no. 27 (1986), p. 3, and, as an example of the problems in a particular place, 'Trudovoe obuchenie uchashchikhsya I-VIII klassov shkol g. Tuly,' Narodnoe obrazovanie no. 11 (1986), p. 99.

23.   The description of the 1 September ceremonies is based on personal attendance at one such, and on Christel Lane, The Rites of Rulers, (CUP, Cambridge, 1981), pp. 94-6.

24.   For further details, see Wendy Rosslyn, 'Peace Education in the Soviet Union,' in Avis, Making of the Soviet Citizen, pp. 161-83.

25.   Details of the curriculum at all levels are to be found in J. Muckle, A Guide to the Soviet Curriculum.

26.   Umansky, p. 60.

27.   V.V. Kraevsky and I. Ya. Lerner, Teoreticheskie osnovy soderzhaniya obshchevo srednevo obrazovaniya (Pedagogika, Moscow, 1983), is the major Soviet work on the theory of the curriculum. It is translated in Soviet Education, vol. 28, nos 8-9 (1986), passim. See also Muckle, Chapter 2 of A Guide.

28.   For a detailed account of observations of Soviet classrooms and an analysis of their characteristic spirit, see J. Muckle, 'Classroom interactions in some Soviet and English schools,' Comparative Education, vol. 20, no. 2 (1984), pp. 237-51. The 'Guidelines' state new requirements for both content and methods of instruction.

29.   J. Muckle, 'Dmitri Kabalevsky and the three whales. Recent developments in music education in the Soviet general education school,' British Journal of Music Education, vol. 4, no. 1 (1987), pp. 53-70.

30.   Further details are contained in two articles by J. Muckle, 'The foreign language teacher in the Soviet Union: observing teachers at work,' Modern Languages vol. 42, no. 3 (1981), pp. 153-63, and 'Modern language teaching in the Soviet Union,' Perspectives, no. 12 (1983), pp. 65-80.

31.   Narodnoe khozyaistvo SSSR v 1985g. (Statistika, Moscow, 1986), p. 30.

32.   Jennifer Louis, 'More testing times under glasnost,' Times Educational Supplement, 24 April 1987, p. 14.

33.   The details in this paragraph are taken from the examination regulations; 'Tipovaya instruktsiya ob ekzamenakh, perevode i vypuske uchashchikhsya obshcheobrazovatelnykh shkol,' Narodnoe obrazovanie, no. 2 (1986), pp. 100-2.

34.   The examination questions for 1987 were issued in pamphlet form: Bilety dlya vypusknykh ekzamenov za kurs 8-letnei shkoly na 1986-87 uchebny god, and Bilety dlya vypusknykh ekzamenov za kurs srednei shkoly na 1986-87

uchebny god, both published by Prosveshchenie, Moscow, 1987.

35.   On the 'humiliation' by teachers of pupils who could achieve marks no better than 3, see 'Educator reviews changes in the schools,' Current Digest of the Soviet Press, vol. 36, no. 39, (1984), pp. 9-10. On the social and economic necessity for change at age 15, see Dunstan 'Soviet education beyond 1984', pp. 164-5.

Chapter Two

GIFTED YOUNGSTERS AND SPECIAL SCHOOLS*

John Dunstan

INTRODUCTION

In my book, Paths to Excellence and the Soviet School, I examined the problems of catering for young people of high and very high ability in the comprehensive education system of the USSR over the period since 1958, particularly up to 1973. (1) There was the background of declining economic growth in an era of accelerating scientific and technological advance and stark international rivalry. There were the consequent imperatives of becoming increasingly self-reliant in matters of research, development and innovation and maintaining as impressive a performance as possible in the great contest in order to foster or sustain in friends or potential friends a belief in the eventual triumph of the cause. All these things intensified the search for educational efficiency for the human material that would constitute the leading cadres of the future.

Opposition to policies that would, in the short term at least, add to inequality was not silenced by denial of such inequality. Nor was it stilled by the argument that temporarily increased inequality was necessary in order to build more speedily the truly equitable society of the future.

*Part of this chapter appeared in an earlier version as 'Die Förderung hochbegabter Kinder in der UdSSR - gegenwärtige Entwicklungen und Probleme,' in Oskar Anweiler and Friedrich Kuebart (eds), Bildungssysteme in Osteuropa - Reform oder Krise? (Berlin Verlag, (West) Berlin, 1984), pp. 154-74. We are grateful to the editors and publishers for their cooperation.

The force of this opposition, whether expressed in terms of social justice - a less common argument at that time perhaps because it was more hazardous - or more often in terms of the spoliation of that same maximal personality development which the advocates of special provision were also apt to invoke, was sufficient to wreck the initiatives of 1958. But it was not enough to prevent in the first half of the 1960s the gradual though limited expansion of special forms of schooling, either for young people of very high ability, e.g. mathematics and physics boarding schools (fiziko-matematicheskie shkoly-internaty or FMShs) or for children likely to include a more than average share of the very able, e.g. language schools, because of demand for places frequently exceeding supply.

Continuing anxieties about character formation and the dangers of a lopsided programme in such schools coalesced with the concerns behind the great curriculum debate of the mid-1960s and the ensuing reforms to furnish new directions for the education of children with special abilities. Cognitive goals now had a much wider remit: not just the favoured few but the mass of clever children were to be catered for. And so the decree of November 1966, while extending legitimation to schools and classes with advanced study of particular subjects, expressed itself somewhat guardedly as to their development - it was permitted to have 'a certain number' (nekotoroe kolichestvo) of such schools - and made it plain that the major vehicle of provision for particular interests and abilities was to be options (elective courses) from form VII, taken in addition to the common basic curriculum. This represented a compromise, theoretically capable of satisfying both supporters and opponents of special provision; but in practice disagreement continued, focused on whether options should be open to all children.

By 1973 the official line might be summed up thus: with the aim of providing suitably for particular abilities, differentiation as between various types of schools had proved itself but needed circumspect handling. Differentiation within the mass school was a good thing, not of course in the sense of dividing pupils into separate classes on the basis of ability, but in the form of optional studies available to all older children deemed capable of profiting from them, and also in that of differentiated teaching methods (flexible and tactful groupings within the mixed-ability class). Opposition continued to manifest itself by way of reluctance or refusal to accept this line, springing no doubt from grounds of principle as well as practicality. It could also be seen in the uninterrupted search for new and improved means of extracurricular and out-of-school provision for special abilities, though, given the exigencies deriving from manpower, geography and climate, it would be wrong to ascribe this solely to egalitarian forces.

It has been estimated, by conflation of Soviet data, that at the beginning of the 1970s special schools of all kinds and schools with special classes, numbering at least 1265, represented no more than 3 per cent of general secondary ten- or eleven-year day schools. (2) Since special schools tend to be smaller than ordinary ones, the proportion of pupils attending them is likely to have been lower still. Schools for the fine arts comprised some 100 (0.23 per cent of all general secondary day schools), sports boarding schools 18 (0.04 per cent), foreign language schools 600 (1.36 per cent), mathematics and physics boarding schools 11 (0.02 per cent), and other schools with intensive teaching of particular subjects 536 (1.21 per cent). (3) By October 1973, optional subjects were being taken by 54 per cent of pupils in the eligible school-years. (4)

In the present study I shall be predominantly concerned with the quantitatively most significant forms of provision for above-average intellectual abilities, namely schools with intensive teaching of particular subjects (called more succinctly special-profile schools) and language schools, and to a lesser extent with options. I shall first offer a brief general impression of the situation in the mid-1970s, then give under various headings an account of trends and discussion up to the eve of the 1984 school reform, attempt to relate the situation during that period to a somewhat wider context, and finally consider subsequent developments up to 1986/87 and some of their implications.

SPECIAL SCHOOLS COME OF AGE

Around the mid-1970s an important series of official documents was issued which testified irrefutably to the fact that in the view of the authorities the special schools and classes had come of age. On 27 December 1973 the RSFSR Minister of Education approved the first 'Regulations on the secondary general school teaching a number of subjects in a foreign language,' (5) although the RSFSR decree forming the legal basis of these schools and cited in the document had been passed more than fourteen years earlier. (6) Then on 18 February 1974 similar approval was given to 'Regulations on schools and classes with intensive theoretical and practical study of particular subjects,' and issued together with an order 'On improving the work of schools and classes with intensive study of particular subjects' dated 22 February, the latter including reference to language schools. (7) Regulations on optional studies followed early in 1975, (8) and those on special sports classes received approval on 3 October 1977. (9)

About this clutch of legislation - and here the first two documents are of particular significance - the following may be said. True, there had been divisions among educationists: we recall the fierce opposition to special schools expressed by V.N. Stoletov, the then President of the Academy of Pedagogical Sciences, early in 1973, (10) and it is unlikely that his was a lone voice. Nevertheless, the legitimation of special schools and classes adumbrated in the November 1966 decree and confirmed in outline in the Legislative Principles on Public Education of July 1973 was now spelt out in detail. This formally set on them the seal of official acceptability.

On the other hand, the issue was still apparently too sensitive to permit the luxury and the possible danger of a renewed public airing. It is quite noticeable how the regulations on special-profile schools stress again and again the ways in which they are to conform to the practices of mass schools, and the same emphasis recurs in a thesis devoted to their problems by V. Golovina. (11) In particular, reduction of the time allotted to specific non-profiled subjects 'could lead to the infringement of the principle of the unity of the Soviet schools.' (12) It is equally noticeable that the first two documents passed unrecorded by the mass educational press, as if deliberately ignored, while the one on options was duly expounded. It is also worth noting that the mathematics and physics boarding schools have acquired no comparably formalised legitimacy and that these more obviously exceptional schools for exceptional young people retain their experimental status with the degree of uncertainty thereby implied. As an illustration of this we may cite the 1978 prospectus of the Novosibirsk FMSh. (13) The latest normative document therein mentioned is dated 1968 and still refers to the FMShs as experimental. Thus, although special schools in general have at last attained their official majority, a few have yet to do so, and even those which have come of age are still subject to growing pains.

TRENDS AND DISCUSSION 1973-1983

Over the period 1973-83 the pains and their causes and cure still found their diagnosticians from time to time, even though discussion was nothing like as frequent as it had sometimes been in the past. It will be surveyed under the headings of distribution, selection, organisational matters, and character education.

Distribution

Special schools and classes tended to be formed without due regard to the social and economic needs of the area. As a rule they were set up only in large towns and mainly in central districts, (14) reducing accessibility for children from workers' settlements and villages, since they seldom possessed boarding accommodation. (15) At the beginning of the 1970s, only 40 of Uzbekistan's 124 new special classes were operating in rural localities, whereas 85 per cent of schools and 70 per cent of pupils were to be found in rural areas, and there was not a single rural class specialising in biology, provision of which with a bias towards agronomy was essential. (16) In the RSFSR, it was claimed, there were very few biology schools and their development was almost at a standstill, whereas more than half of the Republic's special schools were for languages and such a situation was unjustified. (17) But the Russian Ministry of Education called for schools of both kinds, language and special-profile, to be established in big housing estates, workers' settlements, and, given the necessary conditions (presumably residential facilities), in large rural population centres. (18)

It is perhaps worth mentioning at this point that the contribution of the FMShs towards the elimination of the urban-rural gap in educational opportunity continued to be cited as one of the main points in their favour, as indeed it should be as a principal raison d'être. (19) We should also note the Novosibirsk school's success in reducing the sexual imbalance in its pupil numbers to one girl to three boys in

1978-79, though some may be irritated by the Soviet writer's obsession with chivalry and saddened by the girls' conviction that the boys were better at physics. (20) Optional studies were still being commended, but their stipulation of minimum enrolments was said to make them virtually impossible to organise at small country schools, thus adding to urban-rural disparity. (21)

Selection

Faults in distribution were blamed for the fact that the social composition of the pupil body at special schools did not match that of their catchment area. This was expressed in the starkest terms that the present writer can remember encountering; after referring to a 4 per cent or smaller share of workers' children at certain schools in Volgograd, Novosibirsk, Moscow and elsewhere, the RSFSR Ministry of Education order commented that 'the social composition of their pupils does not reflect the current distribution of the children of workers, collective farmers and white-collar employees in the corresponding towns: as a rule the children of white-collar workers comprise 70-80 per cent of the pupil total at foreign language and special-profile schools.' (22) A survey of similar data found that the children of white-collar workers and specialists constituted 58.5 per cent of the population of special schools and 32.5 per cent of ordinary schools (workers' children comprising 34.2 per cent and 50.5 per cent respectively). (23) According to the sociologist Filippov, other research too had shown that in many special schools most of the pupils were children of the intelligentsia. (24) He felt that widening the network and providing residential annexes would solve the problem, but the RSFSR Ministry seemed to imply that more specific intervention was required when it instructed local education authorities and its own inspectorate to keep a check on recruitment to special-profile classes and to ensure their social mix (obespechit raznorodnost ikh sotsialnovo sostava). (25) How this was to be done was not explained; but it was fairly obvious that white-collar and specialist parents were unduly adept at getting their children into such schools.

The Ministry also stated that the local authorities should prevent pupils who were 'not prepared' for special-profile classes from enrolling in them. This indicates other problems of selection. As a rule, the most (generally) able and hard-working were chosen, irrespective of their particular interests and aptitudes, and including some 20 per cent with low marks in the special subjects. A significant proportion did not reveal any aptitudes or abilities in these subjects after arrival in form IX; a mere 8-10 per cent achieved excellent marks, and about half made only moderate progress, many being later required to leave. (26) High ability and diligence were by no means unimportant, but the main thing was that the pupils should already have indicated their potential; local Komsomol committees should interest themselves in the matter and recommend suitable individuals. (27)

The language schools had similar difficulties; indeed, with recruitment at the age of six or seven their chances of determining linguistic potential must be much slighter. Many pupils, the Ministry declared, were moved from forms II-VIII to ordinary schools because of inadequate progress in the foreign language, and a significant number did not embark upon the senior course. (28) A teacher at a language school also told me in the spring of 1979 that some of her pupils turned out to be no good at the foreign language: their lack of enthusiasm caused considerable problems, so they were allowed to drop the subject.

Although disclosures of this kind, official and unofficial, may be somewhat startling, once they are accepted it is no surprise to learn that many pupils from some of the schools choose jobs that have nothing to do with the special subjects. In Volgograd Region, asserted the Russian Ministry of Education, only 1.5 to 3 per cent of language school leavers were in employment connected with the foreign language. Of 27 leavers from form X of a school at Lipetsk specialising in mathematics and computer technology in 1973, not one had chosen the specialism of computer programmer. Not more than 15 per cent of leavers from special classes took up the corresponding specialisms in higher education, and only about 12 per cent went into appropriate jobs. (29) The number of ex-pupils of language schools entering language institutes was also branded insignificant, and those who did so proceed had to follow the same syllabuses as students from ordinary schools, (30) which suggests a waste of potential.

The RSFSR experience, though quantitatively important, is not necessarily applicable to other parts of the USSR. Data from other republics are sparse, but in 1975-6, whereas only 24.9 per cent of pupils completing Lithuania's special classes in the humanities chose related specialisms, 82.2 per cent of those from special mathematics classes did so. (31) And there is another side to the Russian coin too. The majority of pupils completing the form X course were high achievers. Although only a small proportion of students from special schools continued their specialism on entry to higher education, three to five times as many were admitted to other higher education courses. Such pupils' chances of entering higher education were three or four times greater than those at ordinary schools.

Nevertheless the irrationality which the performance of a minority of pupils at special schools introduced into the planning process was sufficient for demands that the situation should be remedied. Efficiency might be increased partly through improved selection and partly through better teaching. As to the former means, local bodies were exhorted to play a more dynamic role in spotting and recommending youngsters with potential for study in special-profile schools. Selection tests were categorically forbidden by the regulations; yet it was obviously felt in some quarters that harder evidence of potential was required than that afforded by the informal interviews held at language schools and the previous academic records considered in the case of candidates for special-profile schools. Scientific testing might furnish such evidence, but there were decades of disrepute to set aside. Even so, in addition to the Western intelligence tests reported by Sutton to have been used fairly recently for survey purposes with handicapped children, (32) the scientific evaluation of abilities seemed to be considered by some to have wider applications, given the limitations of school marks and impressionistic reports. One investigator, for example, used Raven's Progressive Matrices in his work on the relationship between abilities and achievement in a wide range of pupils, and avowed the correct diagnosis of mental abilities to be a prerequisite for using the appropriate means of teaching and upbringing. (33) Academician B.E. Paton, President of the Ukrainian Academy of Sciences, criticised the rejection, without adequate reasons, of tests permitting the determination of pupils' abilities and aptitudes. (34) As to better teaching, let us turn to the discussion on matters pertaining to the internal organisation and operation of the schools.

Organisational matters

In the quest for the raising of the general efficiency of the schools, many of the demanded improvements applied to Soviet schools as a whole, whereas a few had more specific relevance to schools for high-ability children. There was the familiar plea for better teacher training, recruitment and in-service training, including dissemination of the best experience; the need was also expressed for study aids for the pupils and didactic materials for their teachers, commodities in particularly short supply in the languages of the nationalities. While the problems expressed in such general terms were common to special schools and mass schools alike, their solutions of course were not, requiring in the former case specific and probably costlier forms of resource allocation. Formally, special schools were opened by the Republican ministries of education on the application of the regional education authorities; but some Republican ministries gave much more dynamic leadership than others, those of the Baltic Republics being particularly active, (35) witness the fact that half of Estonia's complete secondary schools and one-third of Latvia's possessed special classes at the end of the 1970s. (36)

The main operational problem peculiar to the language schools over the 1970s, according to people involved with them, continued to be that of teaching other subjects through the medium of the foreign language, which had both pedagogical and administrative implications. The 1982 handbook for prospective entrants to higher education still listed five pedagogical institutes offering courses such as mathematics or biology in the English language, though the total number of courses was fewer than in 1969 (nine against sixteen) and the subject spread was somewhat different. (37) However, the head teacher of School No. 169 in Leningrad told me that although his school used to teach geography, physics, chemistry and physical education through English, it had been decided that 'harm was being done' to those subjects, so the practice had been abandoned, geography being the last subject to go over to the medium of Russian in 1976-77. (38) Like others of its kind, the school was now known as a 'school with intensive English teaching' (shkola s uglublyonnym prepodavaniem angliyskovo yazyka). At the Moscow City Education Department (GUNO) I was again informed, by the inspector in charge of these schools, that the main reason why teaching through the foreign language had been dropped was that it was more superficial, although a few experimental schools were still doing it. (39) My remark that I had heard at one of the Moscow schools that it was cost that had brought about the cessation of the practice (40) was not disputed. It is probable that both factors played a part. (41)

Certain problems more specific to special-profile schools were how to find the proper balance between advanced theoretical study and its practical applications, the latter sometimes tending to suffer; (42) when to start the advanced courses; and how to safeguard the position of the non-profiled subjects. When equipment and materials are in short supply, there is a natural temptation to stress theory at the expense of practice. The heavy workload in the profiled subjects led to a call to spread the syllabus more thinly by introducing the intensive course in form VII. (43) Those authorities which moved in this direction by surreptitiously permitting intensive teaching from form VII were, however, implicitly castigated by the RSFSR Ministry of Education. (44) Apart from ideological pressures against academic specialisation in the general school and the consequent tendency to delay this as long as possible, any downward extension of the time devoted to the special subjects, it was argued, would adversely affect the general ones. By calling for an earlier start with the intensive teaching while simultaneously warning against reducing the hours allocated to other subjects, (45) Golovina seems to have wanted to have her cake and eat it. Nevertheless, the earlier specialisation was later to become the norm, following the issue of a USSR Ministry of Education order of 1985.

Mention of general subjects brings us to the matter of character education, but, before turning to this, reference may be made to the mainly organisational problems which were apparently continuing to beset optional subjects. In the RSFSR at least, the range of approved options was rather narrow; their methodological basis was ill-defined, and there was a shortage of ancillary materials; the deciding factor in setting them up was often the teacher's workload; the pupils were sometimes dragooned into joining; and in some schools they were generally regarded as extracurricular work, which meant that they were not taken very seriously and died a premature death. (46) When options received commendation, this tended to refer to a particularly interesting new development such as the course on Family Studies (<u>Osnovy</u>

znaniy o semye) originally tried out as an elective in form IX of 160 Latvian schools, and introduced on a compulsory basis throughout the Republic in 1981. (47) Their position was strengthened, however, by new nationwide regulations which, with just a trace of reluctance, legitimated their long-disputed function of preparing for entry to higher education. (48) Such preparation, involving not only subject matter but also method, had psychological value, reducing the dropout of first-year students. (49)

The effect of taking relevant options on opportunities for higher education (vuz) admission was realistically summed up by an East German commentator. A narrow approach to optional studies, directed only at solving problems in the entrance examinations, had been rejected by the USSR Ministry of Public Education. Indeed, it was maintained that a good mastery of the compulsory material was sufficient for vuz entry. Nevertheless, the extended knowledge of the special field and the influence of elective studies on performance in the obligatory courses did increase the chances of success, and for a large proportion of older pupils their choice of options was of decisive importance. (50)

Character education

'General education in the humanities is very important, as the experience of special schools has shown,' a Leningrad sociologist remarked to me. The reason why the RSFSR statute on special-profile schools stipulated that the non-profiled subjects must follow the ordinary unified syllabuses, and that reduction of time for these was forbidden, (51) and why the Ministry of Education complained of insufficient attention to the quality of teaching in arts subjects at a number of these schools, (52) was that they were deemed to have a particularly important role in such a context in forming the well-rounded socialist personality. Golovina urged that the humanities should have a special place in extracurricular work in these schools; (53) traditional features of upbringing such as socially-useful work, arrangements whereby the academically stronger pupils acted as consultants to the others and Komsomol members helped lagging juniors, and the fostering of a self-critical attitude in the individual child, all acquired particular significance. (54)

The need to be alert to the possibility of one-sided personality development in the children at such schools was to receive additional theoretical backing. They were likely to contain an above-average share of gifted children. The psychologist N.S. Leites, who is probably the foremost living Soviet expert on child giftedness, alluded to the extreme capacity of such children for intellectual imitation and to the satisfaction which they derived from intellectual activity of a highly formalistic kind. This formalism of thinking might be sharply revealed in their moral consciousness, for instance in statements that nobody had any obligations towards his parents. (55) In other words, mental development might outpace moral development, and this was where the educator and the collective had an important therapeutic role.

In the early 1980s the subject of character education in special sports classes received most scrutiny, with the development of these facilities. They were commended for the high level of their training and the sense of purpose and self-discipline which they could instil in their students. But sometimes the 'champions' would titter at the 'weeds'; and if the school gave these youngsters free chocolate and oranges, exempted them from wearing the uniform, allowed them to come in late and released them indiscriminately for away fixtures, it was no wonder that superior attitudes were inculcated. (56) Although the Moscow school here cited seems to have been exceptionally indulgent, and elsewhere the young sportsmen and women might well work hard and get no privileges, the creation of a de facto 'school within a school' and its students' lack of time for other collective activities did suggest to some educators that part-time sports schools and special boarding schools were to be preferred. (57)

THE PERIOD 1973-1983 IN RETROSPECT: SOME QUESTIONS

As we look back, the first question to ask is a quantitative one. To what extent did provision for high-ability children expand over the 1970s? Sadly, the conjunction of information on different types of such provision throughout the USSR that appeared early in the decade seems not to have recurred at its end. The most that can be done is to bring together some fragmentary data. Between 1967-68 and 1971-72 the RSFSR's special-profile schools increased from 200 to 323 and from 1 per cent to 1.5 per cent of its complete secondary schools, while its language schools grew from 266 in 1968-69 to 285 in 1971-72 (constant at about 1.3 per cent, because of the expansion of general secondary education); by 1973-74 the total had dropped from 608 to 542 (2.4 per cent), though language schools had continued to develop; (58) there were probably 298 of them against 244 special-profile schools. (59) Over the period of the Ninth Five-year Plan (1971-1975), the total number of schools with intensive study of individual subjects trebled in the Ukraine, (60) though we cannot say what proportion of complete secondary schools they represented. In Moscow, the number of language schools rose from 76 in 1970-71 (9.3 per cent of complete secondary schools) to 84 in 1978-79 (9.6 per cent) (61) and to 89 in 1980-81 (10 per cent). (62) In Leningrad they numbered 35 (9.3 per cent) in 1971-72 and 50 in 1978-79. (63) The most that can be said with safety is that in some parts of the USSR special schools had increased, but at a modest rate. Against this, 'schools with intensive teaching' other than language schools clearly suffered diminution in terms of countrywide provision. Their share of the school network has been put - authoritatively, but vaguely - at under 1 per cent. (64) I have seen no detailed discussion of this specific trend, but it was attributed to a shortage of suitable staff and facilities, and to unresolved (and latterly unspecified) 'organisational and pedagogical problems'. (65) The Rector of Kharkov University complained of the education authorities' loss of interest in mathematics and physics schools and classes. (66) A shining exception to this unsatisfactory picture, by the mid-1980s at least, was Estonia, where demand was said to be fully satisfied. (67)

Lest the decline be exaggerated, however, it may be as well to reflect on Soviet definitions. Although the earlier-mentioned 3 per cent estimated share of schools of all kinds for special talent and schools with special classes in the total number of general secondary day schools is not conspicuously high, Soviet statistics, which are exceedingly rare in this area, tend to give an even more limited picture. In June 1981, in connection with an international conference on high-ability children, with Soviet participation and thus presumably with Soviet blessing, the Centre International de Recherche et d'Education Prospectives, Paris, issued a figure of 400,000 Soviet children identified as particularly able and given special schooling. (68) This represents 1.24

per cent of pupils at general secondary day schools, or 1.01 per cent of those at all general day schools. (69) A partial explanation of this is that Soviet educationists (and spokespersons) have officially tended to regard language schools and schools with intensive teaching of other subjects not as special schools at all but as forms of external differentiation open to everyone, (70) and thus to exclude them from global statistics. Yet their colleagues and ordinary citizens alike persist in calling them spetsshkoly and in regarding them as special; and so do we.

Undoubtedly special were the sports boarding schools training the country's future Olympic champions and the sports leadership of the constituent Republics (see Chapter 4). After rapid growth in the later 1960s their development became somewhat uneven and by 1977-78 there were 27 of them. By 1983 they had increased to 35, plus five authorised for opening that year by an order of 5 August. Total pupil numbers targeted for the whole USSR were 15,121, (71) representing 0.04 per cent of pupils at general secondary day schools. (72) Varying from 548 to 160, planned enrolments per school averaged 378; the number of sports specialisms ranged from two to eleven, though most schools offered six or seven. Pupil numbers per specialism varied from maxima of 2512 for track and field and 1401 for swimming to minima of 25 for chess and 20 for archery.

Options have developed considerably, if unevenly. The proportion of 54 per cent of eligible pupils noted above for 1973-74 over the whole country had grown to 60 per cent in 1975 or 1976. (73) In Latvia over 60 per cent of them were taking these courses in 1979-80; (74) this is impressive, considering Latvia's tardiness in this respect ten years earlier. (75) By 1983, no fewer than 91.5 per cent of Soviet youngsters in the relevant forms were involved in optional studies. On the debit side, attendance at options in mathematics, physics, chemistry, history and social studies was substantially down on 1973. Lesson periods intended for this purpose continued to fall victim to compulsory subjects, and in rural schools they might be depleted to the point of non-existence. (76)

Can it be concluded from this that the problem of differentiation of the Soviet school system in respect of academic interests and abilities for the sake of the maximalisation of human capital and/or personal development receded from public consciousness over this period, partly perhaps because of deliberate policy and partly because other imperatives crowded it out? I think it can. There was less fundamental questioning of the principle, at least in published form, but then there was far less discussion of the topic then than in the 1960s, even if we interpret it broadly to include differentiated teaching methods within the class.

Since differentiated methods ceased to be controversial some time before and had been officially blessed for several years - though they are hardly yet widespread, it would seem, in the schools - it was not surprising that they did not receive conspicuous attention. The opposition's change of line over this comes across with startling clarity if we juxtapose two pronouncements by V.N. Stoletov, until 1981 President of the USSR Academy of Pedagogical Sciences. In 1973 he declared that 'only by giving all young people identical teaching up to maturity can the problem of abilities and giftedness be objectively solved.' (77) By 1980 he had mellowed sufficiently to say, in a phrase strongly reminiscent of the first Soviet education minister Lunacharsky, 'The teachers' quest is primarily in the direction of selecting suitable methods of teaching appropriate to pupils' potentialities. We should not hold back the growth of those going ahead; we should every day help the backward to overcome their weaknesses.' (78)

This did not mean, however, that egalitarians and differentiators, as I once called them, had forgotten their old hostilities or even called a general truce. The problem might have receded, but it had not disappeared. I sense, though cannot prove, that the discussion of its deeper implications was discouraged at that time, but the question of the desirability of developing the special school network still surfaced occasionally. The sociologist F.R. Filippov's remarks about them in 1974 were very balanced; despite the factual inequality of opportunity of entrance to higher education that their existence created, he nevertheless came down in favour of their expansion in order to mitigate such inequality, for their advantages in training the specialists of the future were indisputable. (79) Conversely, their incipient decline six years later (except for language schools) had 'aggravated the contradictory nature of their social functions.' (80) Academician Paton repeatedly advocated them for children with manifest aptitudes for the natural and technical sciences. (81)

The gulf between the more hard-headed scientists and the more idealistic educationists, which I detected over the issue of special provision in my earlier study - though occupational groups were by no means invariably united within themselves - could still be sensed. Chance comments about these schools heard at research institutes of the Academy of Pedagogical Sciences in the spring of 1979 led me to believe that few eminent educationists really approved of them: 'they are too pleased with themselves,' one observed. V.S. Nazarenko, deputy manager of the Arsenal Works in Kiev, saw what he called their 'excessive proliferation' as a reason why local secondary school pupils shunned jobs in factories such as his own and avoided enrolment in vocational-technical education; and as well as improving vocational guidance and restricting entry to the senior general school course, one of the remedies for this situation would be to cut back the number of special schools. (82) But such public expression of opinion had become rather rare.

It is also arguable that less was heard about special provision for high-ability children by the early 1980s because other curricular concerns had acquired an almost overwhelming dominance. The vocational aspect of Soviet schooling had again come to receive enormous emphasis, and not just since the December 1977 decree. The Legislative Principles of July 1973 saw not only the development of interests and abilities but also the improvement of careers guidance as the aims of special schools and classes and of optional courses; this represented a shift of emphasis from the cognitive to the conative, at least for options, for the statement about the vocational goal replaced one in the 1966 decree about the deepening of knowledge. Although there were occasional complaints as to a lack of actual options in labour training, there was no shortage of publications on how to organise them. Less was printed about the vocational function of special schools.

This prompts another question, and a fundamental one. What, indeed, was the vocational function of special and essentially academic schools and classes at a time when Soviet secondary general education as a whole was becoming increasingly vocationalised? Could and should the special-profile schools retain their primary function of providing well-prepared recruits to higher education, or was there pressure on them to diversify? The current situation was one of some complexity.

On the one hand, it was argued that the traditional function must at all costs be safeguarded. Partly because of the demand for skilled manpower resulting in the promotion of secondary vocational and secondary technical schooling, the competition for entry to full-time higher education had been easing: the total of applications per 100 places (USSR average) had fallen from 269 in 1970 to 255 in 1975, and in the case of industrial vuzy from 232 to 203. By 1980 the reduction in the number of secondary school pupils occasioned by the decline of the birthrate in many areas would further affect this. (83) Relaxation of competition was believed to diminish the likelihood of selecting the most able candidates. But the scientific and economic leadership had yet greater cause for concern: still fewer leavers were applying to technological and natural science faculties because of a flight from mathematics and science to the humanities. (84) Maybe this reflected a certain loss of faith in scientific progress; this was said to be observable among Soviet intellectuals. Maybe the more material fact that a vocational school product with two years' experience earned as much as a research associate with a candidate's degree (85) also had something to do with the shortage of applicants. In these circumstances, many considered the special-profile school to be the best prospect for supplying the rising generation of specialists. Even there, however, where the rate of vuz admissions might be three or four times higher than in the mass school, we find the RSFSR Education Ministry complaining of the small percentage of leavers entering vuzy in the same field.

On the other hand, we are confronted with the paradox that while the Ministry bewailed the failure of most ex-pupils of special schools to follow the most appropriate courses on enrolling in higher education, S.I. Shvartsburd, the educationist responsible for mathematics schools and classes, insisted that they were concerned with pre-vocational training, in an intermediate position between optional studies and technical schools; (86) not only that, he declared that their one-sided orientation on preparing for the vuz was a 'defective aim', and that in the future these schools and classes were to provide more medium specialists, highly-skilled workers for whom there was an increasing need. (87) This may in part have been a reaction to contemporary criticism of the role of special schools in feeding parental ambitions and to warnings of moral danger to their pupils. If Shvartsburd's intentions were to be fulfilled, this would certainly represent a moderation of their function in accordance with the educational spirit of the times; though it would not be so far from that of their forerunners of the early 1960s.

When we turn to consider the vocational function of schools with advanced teaching of a foreign language over the period 1973-1983, the further question arises, with unprecedented forcefulness, as to how far one is really justified in bracketing them together with other special-profile schools, either in general terms or specifically as schools which in practice cater for high-ability children. True, the 1974 regulations linked them together, as did the change of name of the language schools. But although, pace Shvartsburd, the proper function of other special-profile schools was in practice regarded by most people in authority as preparing for 'corresponding specialisms' (88) in higher education - and whether they in general achieved this is a moot point - it was never widely held, officially or unofficially as far as I know, that the language schools were in business mainly to provide the 'language faculties' with recruits. Perhaps a quarter of their tenth-formers did take this path. Their primary function, however, according to official statements, was to give language training to young people as an important subsidiary qualification for all sorts and levels of jobs, from diplomats and technologists to nursery-school teachers and international sleeping-car attendants. So from the official point of view their function was of a special pre-vocational kind, a common prelude to a variety of future occupational themes. The notion of superior intellectual abilities was not intrinsic to this (although de facto selection might well cause it to arise), whereas the different official remit of, and ostensible conditions of entry to, other special-profile schools (with specialisation not from the age of 6 or 7, but 14 or 15 and with proven suitability) presupposed above-average attainment and potential.

How far the official function of language schools matched their actual function is another matter. The precise cachet attached to the post of international sleeping-car attendant is unknown to me, but I have grave doubts whether the schools were besieged by hordes of anxious parents intent on their children becoming nursery-school teachers. Common sense (not to mention commentators) suggests that it was the vuzy that most of them had in mind, even though in these days of change a few of their offspring might develop alternative plans, and a minority would not make the grade anyway. If the Volgograd

Region was at all typical, the language per se would not have been of much importance. I suspect the parents of entrants to other special-profile schools pictured their youngsters in higher education too; here again it seems to have often been the school rather than the specialism which attracted them, but, for some at least, well-defined interests would have suggested higher education of a particular kind.

The idiosyncratic character and role of language schools presented itself to the writer with unusual clarity some time ago through the simple device of counting references to them. Some 382 allusions to specific types of intracurricular provision or potential provision for high-ability children (excluding options) dating from the period 1958-1973 had been amassed, including language schools and schools with a special profile. While the latter accounted for 81 (21.2 per cent) of these, language schools comprised a mere 25 (6.5 per cent), despite their somewhat greater numbers and longer existence. (89) It had long been accepted that their social complexion and its implications as to equality and the formation of the socialist personality gave cause for concern, as was true of most other types of special schools. But this paucity of data lent support to the notion that there had been a concentrated and largely successful attempt to play down the fact of language schools and to minimise the amount of publicity given to them in the press; and this seems not to have applied to other special schools of comparable importance (except at the particular juncture of 1973-74, when Stoletov's above-mentioned tirade against the whole genre was apparently judged inopportune, coming as it did only a few weeks before the issue of the draft Legislative Principles). This in turn suggested that language schools possessed unusually dubious ideological credentials and indeed stood out for this reason like the proverbial sore thumb. As we shall see, however, the virtual silence was not to remain unbroken for long.

GUIDELINES AND GLASNOST

Early in 1983, when the USSR Minister of Education was again making positive reference to differentiation, (90) his Ministry announced that jointly with the Academy of Pedagogical Sciences it was going to examine the research done on special schools and classes and on options. (91) How far they got with their enquiry is not known, but it may well have been overtaken by events. For at the June Plenum of the Soviet Communist Party, Andropov and Chernenko spoke of the need to reform the school, including vocational education; the Politburo subsequently set up a special commission; in January 1984 'Draft Guidelines' for the reform were issued; and after a nationwide debate the approved, emended text was published in April. (92) This fundamental document is of the greatest importance for the future shaping of Soviet education. What the draft might say and the final version might confirm or change about provision for special abilities or even giftedness was crucial. Its supporters may well have been optimistic for Chernenko had referred approvingly to the early detection of individual abilities and talents, though apparently in the context of vocational education, (93) and the USSR Minister of Education had subsequently described the Soviet policy of severely limiting the activity of 'schools with advanced teaching' as pointless. (94) Later in 1983 voices - including that of Professor I. Marenko, the authority on upbringing - had again been heard advocating the differentiation of the senior stage of schooling by specialist tracks. (95)

What the draft did contain on this matter turned out to be a slightly worrying damp squib. With just one sentence in almost two large-format newspaper pages of small print, it stated that pupils in the top four forms of the future (VIII-XI) would be given the opportunity for intensive study of certain subjects of their choice (maths and physics; chemistry and biology; social sciences and humanities) with the help of options. Clearly, differentiation for special talent was not presented as a major focus of the reform. True, electives were not only mentioned, but their primacy as a means of such differentiation might be taken as explicit, in that no alternatives were given; in the legislation of 1966 and 1973 they had shared the field with special schools and classes. What then, some wondered, would be the position of the latter?

Others might share the view of a Moldavian Deputy Minister of Education who found the formulation of this section of the draft 'extremely vague'; he proposed the insertion of a clause to provide for the introduction of differentiated teaching in specialised classes at the senior stage of the general school. (96) The same idea had been advocated, though not for all pupils, by a group of top scientists in a letter to the government newspaper <u>Izvestiya</u> on 27 January, and also, as far as science was concerned, by the important State Committee on Labour and Social Issues. (97) Other scientists seized the opportunity to raise once again the possibility of expanding university schools of the FMSh type. (98) There was a steady trickle of articles and correspondence in the newspaper, mostly in favour of specialisation, though a minority of contributors were hostile. In the event, the final version of the sentence in question was identical to the draft.

So the suspense continued. My own view is that the wording was deliberately vague in order to allow more time for the still controversial question to be thought through and to avoid tying hands with respect to the direction of future legislation. In any case, there were many more urgent problems. Some of these, to be sure, impinged upon special schools. The Guidelines now endowed the secondary general school with a vocational function. The 'schools with intensive teaching of particular subjects' had still to ponder how best to exercise this rather than (or in addition to) the pre-vocational function previously ascribed to them. Some, such as those which, as well as preparing their students for higher education, had trained them to be computer programmers along the way, had been doing this for years, and the schools for the arts were in an analogous position.

It took another sixteen months for the position to be officially clarified. Late in August 1985 the USSR Ministry of Education issued an order 'On model curricula for schools and classes with intensive theoretical and practical study of subjects and with teaching of a number of subjects in a foreign language.' (99) Early in 1986 this was followed by 'Model regulations on schools and classes with intensive theoretical and practical study of academic subjects.' (100) Between them these two documents laid down the ground rules for the organisation of vocational training for special school pupils. The training profiles were to be decided by the executive committees of local soviets and public education departments, taking account of labour power requirements and the availability of teachers and teaching resources. In schools and classes with intensive study of Russian, for example, labour training should be for shorthand and typewriting jobs; in those with intensive physics, for jobs in radio-electronics and electronic engineering; and in those with intensive technical drawing or graphic arts, for jobs in design bureaux, drawing offices, and

decorative and applied art combines. Forms of vocational
training in foreign language schools, however, were not
specified in this way.

A series of model curricula for special schools was
appended to the first of these documents. Since foreign
students of Soviet education typically find such materials to
be fascinating and elusive, a few descriptive and
comparative comments may be in order. The difference
between the curriculum for language schools and that for
ordinary ones was that in the former the language course
was to begin three years earlier, with two weekly periods in
form II (seven-plus entry) according to the new numbering,
three in III, and four in IV. In the subsequent forms, the
periods assigned to the foreign language were as follows
(compare those for ordinary schools in brackets): in V, six
(4); in VI, six (3); in VII, five (2); in VIII, six (2); and in IX to
XI, four (1) each. It is noteworthy that even in these schools
only four language periods a week were provided in the last
three years, hardly intensive study. Against this, the number
of periods for options in each applicable year (forms VII to
XI) was only half that in mass schools. Schools specialising
in an oriental language provided a compulsory European one
as well; in common with schools specialising in other
subjects, they offered options only in the top two forms and
for one weekly period only. (101)

Schools with other specialisms were to give extra
teaching in a specific subject or subjects to forms VIII to XI.
The specialisms comprised Russian language; literature;
mathematics; history and social studies; geography; physics;
biology; chemistry; technical drawing; and art. In subjects
not included in the specialism, and in all compulsory
subjects for years 1 to VII, the ordinary school curriculum
was followed. (102)

What were the main differences from the previous
special curricula issued in 1979 and effective from 1980-81?
For the language schools, these were very little, and mainly
explicable by the changes in the ordinary school which had
affected them too: the complete new year for children of
six-plus, an extra period here and there for half or all the
year, and the new subjects Principles of Information Science
and Computer Technology, Ethics and Psychology of Family
Life, and The World Around Us (Oznakomlenie s okruzhay-
ushchim mirom). The large amount of compulsory time
appended as 'socially-useful productive labour', of course,
made a big difference, exactly as it did for the mass school;

but while the ordinary school's allocation for options - totalled Soviet-style from form VII (with two weekly periods) to the top of the school (with four) - had risen merely from 13 periods to 14, options in the language school now jumped from one period a week for the old forms IX and X in 1980 to one per week for the new forms VII to IX and two for the new forms X and XI, a cumulative increase from two to seven. (103)

It was, however, the other special schools and classes that showed the most striking changes. Whereas in 1980 their distinctive curricula had covered the two senior forms only (then IX and X), now they were provided for the last two years of the middle stage as well, i.e. from the new form VIII (entry at 13-plus). (104) This was extremely interesting. It obviously meant that the existing special schools were to be differentiated even more from ordinary ones without any specialisms. But what it might well also mean was that this was, after all, going to be the way in which pupils in forms VIII to IX would be able to study intensively particular subjects of their choice with the help of options, even though the Guidelines avoided mentioning any extension of the special schools network despite lobbying to that end.

A strong pointer to this was suggested by the unusual phraseology of Deputy Minister of Education F. Panachin when first announcing the new curricula; he referred to 'schools with intensive (optional) study of particular subjects of pupils' choice in forms VIII-XI.' (105) At the time, this seemed to relate more to the vague provisions in the Guidelines than to the existing arrangements for special schools and classes. But the new curricula themselves and the subsequent regulations for the institutions offering them came to be couched in virtually the same terms as in 1979: 'schools (classes) with intensive theoretical and practical study of subjects.' (The 1979 circular had spoken of 'study of a number of subjects', but the new regulations made it clear that schools might have a single specialism or different ones.) The options would 'help' insofar as time that would otherwise have been allocated to them would be added to the time devoted to the specialism. To sum up, it looked as if special schools and classes were given the green light for expansion after all.

Meanwhile, at the USSR Academy of Pedagogical Sciences research was under way on curricula and syllabuses for special schools and classes. Already in December 1984 it was said to be working out 'advanced courses' ('kursy povyshennovo urovnya') for senior forms in all the general subjects. (106) The Academy's Five-year Plan for 1986-1990 was to include, as well as syllabuses and ancillary material for options courses, a new curriculum for schools with intensive study of particular subjects, 'providing for the differentiation of teaching in accordance with the pupils' abilities.' (107) The Model Regulations had made it clear that the special teaching was to comprise two stages. In forms VIII and IX, the aim would be to deepen the content of the basic course and apply it more thoroughly, using the standard textbooks plus supplementary literature. At the senior stage there would be increased breadth as well as depth in both theory and applications; special textbooks and additional materials would be used and 'creative assignments' completed. (108)

Generally, therefore, in the two years following approval of the Guidelines the prospects for the development of special schools and classes seemed to have become quite bright after all. But the serenity was about to be shattered. During 1986-87, as part of M.S. Gorbachov's restructuring drive, the terms glasnost (openness) and sotsialnaya spravedlivost (social justice) came to be increasingly invoked. At the January 1987 CPSU Plenum, for example, Gorbachov said 'Restructuring means vigorously ridding society of any distortions of socialist morality, consistent enforcement of the principles of social justice, harmony between words and deeds ...' (109) About this time, special schools in general, and to a much greater extent language schools in particular, were quite suddenly to find themselves the objects of glasnost and the hunting ground for sotsialnaya spravedlivost, or rather the lack of it.

The searchlight was focused initially on a special music school in Tashkent, and by extension to all special schools, in an article in the young people's magazine Sobesednik in September 1986, (110) and on language schools in articles in the newspapers Sovetskaya Rossiya and Moskovskaya pravda in February 1987. (111) The two latter appeared just after a Deputy Minister of Education, speaking about the new draft statute on the general school, had told his foreign listeners, 'Great attention is being devoted to developing the individual abilities of children. Schools and classes with emphasis on individual subjects, fields of knowledge, the arts and types of sport are being set up.' (112) And it at once became clear that there had been attempts to stifle debate.

The Moskovskaya pravda writer claimed that he had been told many times by Party workers and teachers at special schools, 'It's not for you to raise this problem, and what's the point? You'll only irritate important comrades.' (113) A Sovetskaya Rossiya reader asked the rhetorical question, 'Is it really accidental that it is precisely special schools which most frequently prove to be the "zones most closed from criticism", and letters and reports about the disorders and unseemly behaviour occurring there - very often, unfortunately - are checked with the least zeal?' (114) Now, however, the lid was at last raised. We shall briefly review the discussion under the same headings as for the 1970s: distribution, selection, organisational matters and character education.

Distribution

The catchment area system of special schools, particularly language schools, encountered severe criticism. The existing arrangement was that parents living in the school's microdistrict were formally entitled to send their children to it, and only after they had been satisfied could the remaining places be made available to youngsters resident elsewhere. (115) In theory there seems to have been a 20 per cent ceiling on the latter category, (116) but it was often disregarded - being 50 per cent in Vilnius, for example (117) - so that in practice the vast majority of children might be commuters. An important consequence of this policy was that language schools tended to be clustered in more central districts. In Moscow there were seven in both the Krasnopresnensky and the Oktyabrsky Districts, immediately west and south-west of the Kremlin and 'largely populated by the families of people working in ministries and authorities', but none at all in the big (and mainly working-class) Krasnogvardeisky and Sovetsky Districts, (118) on the southern periphery.

There were people who wanted to solve the problem of the irregular distribution of language schools by closing down those that existed. Other contributors to the debate, however, disclaimed such a final solution; one argued that since the mass schools were not teaching foreign languages efficiently this would amount to deliberate reduction of the educational level of the rising generation, and since the intelligentsia would then take on private language teachers

she queried whether society would become more just. (119)
The real answer was to expand the language school network
so as to give equal opportunities to all, and then the system
of admission by microdistrict could and should be rigidly
enforced. (120) Enrolments to other special-profile schools
were independent of the microdistrict principle anyway.
(121)

Selection

The tendency for special schools to be urban and, in big
cities, to be situated centrally in districts favoured by the
intelligentsia had obvious implications for their social
composition. The competitive entry to Special School No.
31, a language school in Moscow's Krasnopresnensky
District, was alleged to be on the basis of parental positions.
Only 6 per cent of the first-year pupils were workers'
children; by the top year they comprised only 3.7 per cent,
and in some schools there were none at all. (122) Other
language schools in Moscow had not a single child of
working-class parents, but the proportion with fathers and
mothers employed in ministries and in management at
district level was more than significant; 25 per cent of first-
formers at School No. 30, for example, were the offspring of
the district leadership. (123)

Soviet apologists have argued that it is not
unreasonable for a special school's social composition to
reflect that of its catchment area, even when neither are
predominantly working-class. That would be all very well if
the special-schoolgoing population reflected the schoolgoing
population citywide. Locational factors alone were enough
to explain that this was not the case. But other factors were
present which made matters worse. Complaints surfaced
that certain language schools were refusing to accept the
children of 'ordinary' ('neprestizhnye') parents. (124) But
what of those who were accepted - and the commuter
children in particular? It was the deputy head of one of
Moscow's special French schools who spilt the beans. There
were three categories of 'illegally admitted' pupils, she said.
There were the children of parents who had moved
elsewhere. (This is not particularly heinous, and indeed the
present writer always believed it to be perfectly
legitimate.) There were the children of former pupils. (We
came across this practice on a visit to Tbilisi in September

1984; in Georgia one takes such phenomena in one's stride, but it evidently occurs elsewhere too.) Then there were the 'pozvonochniki' or 'phone-call children' (the Russian word also means 'backbones', but an appropriate English pun eludes us). (125)

There would appear to be a whole lore of 'pozvonochniki'. The phenomenon is said to date mainly from the 1970s, when special schools began to come increasingly under official scrutiny. (126) Essentially, these children were forced upon the school by a phone-call, letter or word in the ear from higher authority. The agent would usually be the inspector responsible for the school; even if she were to refuse, the parent would probably go over her head. Special schools resented having to take 'pozvonochniki' on three counts: they had to be taken even if the classes were full; they had to be taken irrespective of their stage of development (even if they were backward?); and they were troublesome, playing parental rank. No harm would be done, the teacher mildly yet pointedly remarked, if communist parents were to be reminded about personal responsibility. (127) Another writer maintained that the problem would disappear if high standards were systematically required. (128) Such ideal though obvious counsels could have little impact in the real world.

Yet however haphazard the process of admission to language schools might inevitably be, it must be said that their overall record in preparing for entry to higher education had improved somewhat by the mid-1980s, compared to the mid-1970s position mentioned earlier. An average of 50 to 55 per cent of their final-year pupils now proceeded to technical vuzy, and a further 16 to 18 per cent went on to the language faculties of universities and institutes. Indeed this was slightly up on a sample survey of 1968, with 65.7 per cent vuz entry, though the two sub-totals were reversed in importance. (129) The latter fact might have been a reflection of the mid-1970s data that many of the language-school pupils turned out to have little flair for languages, and of the much more recent claim that the level of the intensive language teaching in these schools had fallen drastically of late. (130) Languages apart, however, if there has been a countrywide decline of interest in higher education, as is frequently alleged, special schools as bastions of such aspirations might well be expected to sustain or even improve their record in these circumstances.

But the general thrust of discussion about career paths

was different from that of the early to mid-1970s, when faults in selection were blamed for special school pupils' failure to continue in their specialisms. It now focused on their failure to enter vocational schools (PTUs). This topic had been absent from the earlier debate, when the only alternative to the vuz was seen, if at all, in terms of specialised secondary (medium technical) education. The emergence of the PTU as a desirable follow-up for language school-leavers would seem utterly bizarre, but for the ethos of the 1984 reform. The doubling of the proportion of 15-year-olds proceeding from general to vocational schooling was suddenly heralded, and great efforts were made - with some success - to boost the appeal of the PTUs. When in 1984, for the first time for years, one pupil in four from this age-group entered a vocational school and the PTU admissions plan was overfulfilled, the teachers' newspaper proclaimed that this reflected 'a turning point in the consciousness of the youngsters themselves, their teachers, and of course their parents.' (131)

The opinion soon began to be voiced that it was somehow shameful for the language schools to be sending none or extremely few of their pupils to the PTUs. (132) During the period 1984-1986, only 3.4 per cent of those completing forms VIII and X of these schools in Moscow had entered PTUs, and a mere 1.8 per cent had gone into jobs in material production. (133) The deputy head of the French school, however, defended such schools against the charge. Why should they send their students to PTUs or working-class jobs, when people with knowledge of a foreign language were better going into the services sector? Teachers at special schools had in fact long spoken of the need to have PTUs which took language training into account, but to no avail. (134) This was a fair point and we have not noticed any rejoinder to it.

Organisational matters

In the area of organisation, the debate showed both continuity and change. The problem of overloading remained on the agenda but attention was now centred on special music schools. The music teaching and practice took up so much time and effort that the general subjects suffered. The USSR Ministry of Culture, bearing overall administrative responsibility for the schools, claimed that it

wanted syllabuses for these subjects to be adapted to the
particular conditions there, but that the Ministry of
Education would not agree to this. The head teacher of the
Central Music School in Moscow asserted, however, that
variants of adapted syllabuses in mathematics, chemistry
and biology were to be discussed and tried out, but the
Ministry of Culture did not consider the matter urgent.
Meanwhile, the health of 40 per cent of the pupils there was
below par. (135)

It will be recalled that one of the topics of discussion
ten years earlier had been the possibility of reducing the
workload at the senior stage of special-profile schools (other
than language schools) by introducing the intensive course
two years sooner, in form VII. We also saw that the Ministry
of Education did an about-turn on this in 1985, and the
earlier start became standard. With the opening-out of the
debate on language schools, some began to call for the
extension of something like the standard special-profile
pattern to these schools also, not however because of
overloading, but for another set of reasons. Perceived to
offer something different and better, they were compelled
legally and illegally to admit a number of children who
turned out to have no bent for the foreign language. This
impeded their official function, and if the problem had been
worsening of late it would explain why the level of
specialised teaching had greatly declined. Early in 1987,
then, it was being suggested that all children should be
taught a foreign language from an early age, and the good
linguist should be picked out for intensive training in special
classes after either the primary or the middle stage. (136)
These classes could be organised in any urban school, or
perhaps those with most experience in teaching the
language.

The quality and supply of teachers for language schools
was not much discussed, and neither was the question of
teaching other subjects through the foreign tongue. The
number of institutions offering such training dropped from
five in 1982 to three in 1983 and two in 1985, when the
Lenin Pedagogical Institute in Moscow provided biology in
English or French and the Ushinsky Pedagogical Institute in
Yaroslavl listed mathematics and physics in English or
French. (137) If there were others, they were not readily
identifiable from the official handbook. Given this apparent
continuation of policy and shrinkage of demand, reflected
also in the use of the new term 'schools with intensive

foreign language teaching' in Moscow in 1979, it was curious to find the Ministry of Education order on model curricula persistently describing them as 'teaching a number of subjects in a foreign lanugage.' (138) Either this was due to inertia, or perhaps to a lingering need to assert the distinctiveness of language schools; but thanks to glasnost, that selfsame distinctiveness was soon to become a definite liability. This was particularly the case when a special school, cheek by jowl with an ordinary one, possessed incomparably superior furnishings and facilities thanks to the patronage of a wealthy sponsoring enterprise or organisation, quite possibly situated outside the district altogether. (139)

Character education

It is indeed interesting that our source described one such enterprise as the school's pokrovitel (patron, with somewhat pejorative undertones) rather than the usual shef (sponsor). This lavish treatment - beautiful workshop and swimming pool, own kitchen - was not the only feature of special schools to have unfortunate implications for character education. Their social composition, inordinately represent- ative of the intelligentsia and containing an awkward component of 'phone-call children', was another. One investigative journalist drew attention to the number of official cars setting down children outside special schools, or farther along the street ... 'So this is how parents give their children lessons in immorality and stress their membership of a special circle. At the same time they love to talk about social justice when among their subordinates at work.' (140) Another enquiry, into the sacking of an allegedly incompetent chemistry teacher from the Uspensky Music School in Tashkent at the instigation of a group of senior girls with the support of their Komsomol organiser, revealed a dreadful collective egotism in the pupils concerned. This was fed by the school management's attitude towards chemistry as a general subject tailor-made for officially permitted absences for concerts or rehearsals, excessive tutelage exemplified in a staff-pupil ratio higher than one to two, and a lack of contact with the outside world apart from concerts (which were resoundingly applauded). (141) The two Moscow journalists went even further in their exposure of the lack of effective character training at language schools, referring to petty trading and thieving within the schools and to crimes of theft and assault outside them, with pupils landing up in the hands of the police or at sobering-up stations. (142)

Not only was this excoriation of the level of upbringing at special schools much franker than ever before, indicting the well-heeled parents also, but there was much more of it and it was more at the heart of the debate. Under the banner of social justice, more and more attacks were made on manifestations of elitism ('<u>elitarnost</u>', usually in inverted commas as if to underline the inappropriateness of this essentially bourgeois phenomenon in the Soviet context). In the 1970s the word had seldom appeared in print, but gradually it came to be heard from people's lips. A schoolboy, writing at the turn of 1981-82, commented 'We have a very ordinary school, it's certainly no "<u>spets</u>", there's nothing "elitist" - as they say nowadays - about it.' (143) Elitism, it was maintained, was what distinguished a special school from an ordinary one; (144) it 'infected' quite a lot of the pupils at language schools. (145) It applied where the main criterion for admitting a child was the parents' place of work. Other kinds of special school, however - such as for mathematics - might merit the elitist label. Even an ordinary school might be elitist if it possessed the reputation of being the premier school in the town; there was such a school in Gorky, literally No. 1, which everyone knew was attended by the children of the city authorities. (146)

CONCLUDING REMARKS

Theoretically, and despite the related 'contradiction' of better life-chances, there is every reason to secure the maximum development of abilities provided that in the first place there exists a societal demand for them. Thus there are no Soviet sports boarding schools specialising in cricket - the very idea is ludicrous - whereas a Moscow secondary general school has been developing the advanced study of aircraft construction. (147) Individual abilities and needs are to be recognised as far as possible, but are subordinate to the requirements of society: this sums up the Soviet position. However much or little one likes it, one does not have to be a Marxist to appreciate the good sense of it in the real world in which politicians operate and educators educate. For more children who are gifted and talented to realise their potential, there must obviously be investment in teacher education, accommodation and equipment, with more emphasis than heretofore on applied science, and positive discrimination in underprivileged localities. On this most Soviet and Western supporters of gifted education would cordially agree, although in the USSR the deprived areas are most likely rural. The common basic problem, of course, is the allocation of resources, though here too there are differences: if in the West there is a widespread lack of funds, in the USSR there is a general shortage of labour power and materials. In these circumstances, social demand or national need is the only criterion likely to carry weight in the corridors of power. To paraphrase Robert Lowe's popularised dictum: we must educate our paymasters, and our quartermasters.

This particular process of education, however, is far from smooth when the needs of a minority are in competition with a mass interest. It may be the enforced partial rundown of an entire education system as in some Western countries which militates against minority claims, or it may be the paramount and all-pervasive demand for the replenishment of the skilled labour force as in the USSR which tends to eclipse other societal needs. To make matters worse, during such unpropitious periods the contradiction of superior life-chances as the probable consequence of special provision for children of high ability is likely to appear particularly glaring. To illustrate this again from history, it was not until Khrushchov's polytechnical reform was already in decline (except for a limited number of special schools) that differentiation of the school structure for the sake of academic abilities enjoyed its modest take-off in a significantly more favourable public climate. The fundamental dilemma is that from the official Soviet point of view the contradiction can only be resolved by making special provision much more widely available; but, apart from the resources problem, those with whom the contradiction carries most weight reject a solution which they perceive as leading - and not necessarily in the short term alone - to an exacerbation of inequality.

And when equality of access to education is cited at the highest level - by Gorbachov at the 27th Party Congress in February 1986 - under the rubric of social justice; and communists are bidden to 'observe the norms of socialist communal life which are the same for everyone' and to 'judge everything openly'; and the top Party leadership of Moscow is accused of complacency and that of Uzbekistan of corruption ('violation of socialist legality'): (148) it is not surprising that some of the resented sacred cows of Soviet education should be called out for slaughter. True, they show no signs of dumbly obeying. But at least we may see their sheds being put in order, unless the priestly stockmen lack the will or the power to act.

NOTES

1.   John Dunstan, Paths to Excellence and the Soviet School (NFER Publishing Company, Windsor, 1978). For a more recent study examining the problem in greater breadth than the present paper seeks to do, see the writer's 'Equalisation and differentiation in the Soviet school 1958-85: a curriculum approach', in John Dunstan (ed.), Soviet Education under Scrutiny (Jordanhill College Publications, Glasgow, 1987), pp. 32-69.

2.   Dunstan, Paths to Excellence, p. 250. If all general day schools are included, the proportion falls to below 1 per cent.

3.   Unit totals (passim in ibid.) set against totals for general day schools in Narodnoe obrazovanie, nauka i kultura v SSSR (hereafter NONK) (Statistika, Moscow, 1977), pp. 26-7.

4.   M.P. Kashin, 'Ob itogakh perekhoda sovetskoi shkoly na novoe soderzhanie obshchevo obrazovaniya,' Sovetskaya pedagogika, 1976, no. 3, p. 30; cited in Dunstan, Paths to Excellence, p. 186.

5.   'Polozhenie o srednei obshcheobrazovatelnoi shkole s prepodavaniem ryada predmetov na inostrannom yazyke,' Sbornik prikazov i instruktsiy Ministerstva prosveshcheniya RSFSR (hereafter SPMP), 1974, no. 5, pp. 29-32.

6.   'O poryadke i srokakh perekhoda na novuyu sistemu shkolnovo obrazovaniya,' 7 Aug. 1959 (ibid., p. 29).

7.   'Ob uluchshenii raboty shkol i klassov s uglublennym izucheniem otdelnykh predmetov,' SPMP, 1974, no. 11, pp. 2-7; 'Polozhenie o shkolakh i klassakh s uglublennym teoreticheskim i prakticheskim izucheniem otdelnykh uchebnykh predmetov,' ibid., pp. 8-11.

8.   Uchitelskaya gazeta, 28 Jan. 1975.

9. 'Polozhenie o spetsializirovannykh klassakh po vidam sporta s prodlennym dnem obucheniya v obshcheobrazovatelnykh shkolakh,' SPMP, 1978, no. 1, pp. 23-7.

10. Uchitelskaya gazeta, 15 Feb. 1973.

11. V.D. Golovina, Vzaimosvyaz obucheniya i vospitaniya v shkole s uglublyennym izucheniem matematiki (NII SiMO APN SSSR, Moscow, 1978), pp. 11, 16. (Author's abstract of thesis.)

12. Ibid., p. 11.

13. Novosibirskaya spetsializirovannaya fiziko-matematicheskaya shkola-internat No. 165 pri NGU. Prospekt (Novosibirsk, 1978).

14. 'Ob uluchshenii,' p. 4.

15. F.R. Filippov, 'Sotsiologicheskie problemy obrazovaniya v SSSR,' Sotsiologicheskie issledovaniya, 1974, no. 2, p. 20.

16. I.K. Kadyrov, 'O rabote shkol i klassov s uglublennym izucheniem otdelnykh predmetov v Uzbekskoi SSR,' in Vsesoyuznaya nauchnoprakticheskaya konferentsiya po probleme uchebno-vospitatelnoi rabote v shkolakh i klassakh s uglublennym izucheniem otdelnykh predmetov (MP SSSR/NII SiMO APN SSSR, Moscow, 1972), pp. 6-12, at pp. 9-10.

17. Filippov, 'Sotsiologicheskie problemy obrazovaniya v SSSR,' p. 20.

18. 'Ob uluchshenii,' p. 6.

19. E.g., A.N. Kolmogorov, I.T. Tropin and K.V. Chernyshev, 'Zabotyas o dostoinom popolnenii,' Vestnik vysshei shkoly, 1974, no. 6, p. 28; Literaturnaya gazeta, 1 Aug. 1979.

20. Literaturnaya gazeta, 1 Aug. 1979; cf. Dunstan, Paths to excellence, p. 127.

21. F.R. Filippov, Sotsiologiya obrazovaniya (Nauka, Moscow, 1980), p.99.

22. 'Ob uluchshenii,' p. 4.

23. Vysshaya shkola kak faktor izmeneniya sotsialnoi struktury razvitovo sotsialisticheskovo obshchestva (Nauka, Moscow, 1978), p. 65.

24. Filippov, 'Sotsiologicheskie problemy obrazovaniya v SSSR,' p. 20.

25. 'Ob uluchshenii,' pp. 6, 7.

26. Ibid., pp. 2-3.

27. V. Barkun, 'V pomoshch spetsializirovannoi shkole,' Komsomolskaya zhizn, 1974, no. 10, pp. 22-4.

28.   'Ob uluchshenii,' p. 3.
29.   Ibid., pp. 3-4. It is not absolutely clear whether the last sentence refers to the Lipetsk school or to special classes in general.
30.   Filippov, 'Sotsiologicheskie problemy obrazovaniya v SSSR,' p. 20; Vysshaya shkola, p. 65.
31.   R. Norkyavichene, 'K probleme komplektovaniya klassov s uglublennym izucheniem otdelnykh predmetov,' in Rol fakultativnykh zanyatiy v opredelenii soderzhaniya i metodov obucheniya v shkole budushchevo (NII SiMO APN SSSR, Moscow, 1978), pp. 115-17, at p. 117.
32.   Andrew Sutton, 'Backward children in the USSR: an unfamiliar approach to a familiar problem,' in Jenny Brine, Maureen Perrie and Andrew Sutton (eds), Home, School and Leisure in the Soviet Union (George Allen and Unwin, London, 1980), pp. 160-91, at p. 181.
33.   A. Lunge, 'O svyazi sposobnosti k rassuzhdeniyu s uspevaemostyu,' in Voprosy pedagogicheskoi psikhodiagnostiki (NII pedagogiki ESSR, Tallinn, 1976), pp. 55-70, at p. 69. Incidentally, he refers (p. 60) to a school in Tartu which selects its pupils on the basis of tests (ispytaniya).
34.   Uchitelskaya gazeta, 2 Apr. 1977.
35.   Dieter Hetsch, Uber Spezialklassen und -schulen als Form der Differenzierung im Schulsystem der UdSSR (Volk und Wissen Verlag, (East) Berlin, 1973), p. 27.
36.   Discussion at Estonian Ministry of Education, Tallinn, 30 Mar. 1979; M. Karklin, 'Latviyskaya SSR,' Narodnoe obrazovanie, 1980, no. 4, p. 28.
37.   Spravochnik dlya postupayushchikh v vysshie uchebnye zavedeniya SSSR v 1982 godu (Vysshaya shkola, Moscow, 1982), pp. 176, 179, 181, 190, 191. For 1969 see Dunstan, Paths to Excellence, p. 106 and note 85 p. 114.
38.   Discussion at the school, 23 Mar. 1979.
39.   Discussion with Mrs V. Ionova, 10 Apr. 1979. Foreign language typing and technical translation are still quite common as labour training.
40.   Discussion with deputy head, 5 Apr. 1979.
41.   I have the impression that Soviet educators feel some compunction about referring to cost as a reason for cutback or lack of expansion. Although in my earlier study I noted the possibility of this inhibiting the growth of the FMShs, I then found no reference to it as a problem (Dunstan, Paths to Excellence, p. 138). But a recently located monograph from the GDR, based on fieldwork, cites 'great expense' as one of the two main difficulties facing the

FMShs, the other being the reluctance of university staff to take on additional work and the consequent inferior substitution of overworked and inexperienced students (Hetsch, Uber Spezialklassen, pp. 43-4, 66).

42. 'Ob uluchshenii,' pp. 3, 5; S.I. Shvartsburd, 'Matematicheskaya spetsializatsiya kak sostavnaya chast sistemy povyshennoi matematicheskoi podgotovki uchashchikhsya,' in Vsesoyuznaya nauchno-prakticheskaya konferentsiya (see note 16 above), pp. 13-19, at p. 18; Norkyavichene, 'K probleme komplektovaniya,' p. 116.

43. Golovina, Vzaimosvyaz, pp. 8, 16.
44. 'Ob uluchshenii,' p. 4.
45. Golovina, Vzaimosvyaz, p. 11.
46. Uchitelskaya gazeta, 24 June 1978.
47. Uchitelskaya gazeta, 26 Mar. 1981.
48. Uchitelskaya gazeta, 19 Sep. 1981.
49. A.A. Alov, 'Individualizatsiya obucheniya i fakultativnye zanyatiya (nekotorye sotsialnye problemy),' in Rol fakultativnykh zanyatiy, pp. 5-8, at p. 8.
50. Gerd Joachim Saro, 'Aspekte der Studienvorbereitung sowjetischer Mittelschüler,' Vergleichende Pädagogik, 1981, no. 4, pp. 352-67, at p. 359.
51. 'Polozhenie o skholakh,' SPMP, 1974, no. 11, p. 10.
52. 'Ob uluchshenii,' p. 5.
53. Golovina, Vzaimosvyaz, p. 11.
54. Barkun, 'V pomoshch spetsializirovannoi shkole,' p. 22; Golovina, Vzaimosvyaz, pp. 12, 15.
55. N.S. Leites, 'Odaryonnye deti,' in A.A. Smirnov (ed.), Psikhologiya i psikhofiziologiya individualnykh razlichiy (Pedagogika, Moscow, 1977), pp. 54-64, at pp. 61-3.
56. Uchitelskaya gazeta, 14 Oct. 1982 and 19 Feb. 1983.
57. Uchitelskaya gazeta, 16 Dec. 1982 and 19 Feb. 1983.
58. For 1967-68, Dunstan, Paths to Excellence, pp. 96 and 159; for subsequent years, Vysshaya shkola, p. 64; later percentages derived from NONK, p. 32. This is the most likely interpretation of conflicting data; another source (SPMP, 1974, no. 11, p. 2) seems to apply the 1971-72 figures to 1973-74.
59. There were 66 fewer special schools in 1973-74 than in 1971-72, but according to Vysshaya shkola, p. 64, special-profile schools were 79 fewer. Therefore 13 additional language schools must have been set up. There is no suggestion that special schools for the visual and

performing arts are also involved here.

60. V. Usenko, 'Razvitie shkolnovo obrazovaniya na Ukraine,' Narodnoe obrazovanie, 1977, no. 10, pp. 18-22, at p. 21.

61. For 1970-71, Dunstan, Paths to Excellence, pp. 96 and 111; for 1978-79, discussion with Mrs Ionova at GUNO, 10 April 1979. According to Saro, 'Aspekte der Studienvorbereitung sowjetischer Mittelschüler', p. 361, the 84 schools comprised 52 for English, 15 for German, 14 for French, and 3 for Spanish; in addition there were six special boarding schools.

62. Uchitelskaya gazeta, 2 July 1981; percentages derived from Moskva v tsifrakh, 1980 (Statistika, Moscow, 1980), p. 161.

63. Dunstan, Paths to Excellence, p. 111; discussion with head of School no. 169, 23 March 1979.

64. V.M. Monakhov and V.A. Orlov, 'Uglublennoe izuchenie otdelnykh predmetov,' Sovetskaya pedagogika, 1986, no. 9, pp. 31-33, at p. 33.

65. Filippov, Sotsiologiya obrazovaniya, p. 99.

66. Pravda, 12 Nov. 1982.

67. M.A. Prokofiev, 'Fakultativnye zanyatiya: perspektivy razvitiya,' Sovetskaya pedagogika, 1986, no. 9, pp. 27-30, at p. 29.

68. Erwin Hilgendorf, Die Förderung besonders befähigter Schüler in der Sowjetunion (Pädagogisches Zentrum, (West) Berlin, 1985), p. 123.

69. Calculated from Narodnoe khozyaistvo SSSR v 1980 godu (Finansy i statistika, Moscow, 1981), p. 456.

70. Hilgendorf, Die Förderung, pp. 49-50, citing Danilow and Skatkin, Didaktik der Oberschule (Volk und Wissen Verlag, (East) Berlin, 1978).

71. 'A new source on Soviet sports boarding schools,' Soviet Education Study Bulletin, vol. 2, no. 2 (1984), pp. 63-4; calculated from 'O komplektovanii na 1983-84 uchebny god i ob otkrytii novykh shkolinternatov sportivnovo profilya,' Byulleten normativnykh aktov Ministerstva prosveshcheniya SSSR (hereafter BNA), 1983, no. 11, pp. 36-45.

72. Calculated from Narodnoe khozyaistvo SSSR v 1983 godu (Finansy i statistika, Moscow, 1984), p. 487.

73. Axel Wilske, 'Stand, Probleme und Entwicklungstendenzen des fakultativen Unterrichts in der UdSSR,' Vergleichende Pädagogik, 1978, no. 1, pp. 50-5, at p. 52, citing M.P. Kashin and D.A. Epshtein (eds),

Fakultativnye zanyatiya v srednei shkole, 2nd edn. (Pedagogika, Moscow, 1976).

74.   Karklin, Latviyskaya SSR,' p. 28.

75.   At 17.4 per cent she had been quite atypical of the Baltic republics in 1969 (Dunstan, Paths to Excellence, p. 186).

76.   Monakhov and Orlov, 'Uglublyennoe izuchenie otdelnykh predmetov,' p. 31.

77.   Dunstan, Paths to Excellence, p. 199, citing Obshchestvo i molodyozh (2nd edn., Moscow, 1973) - emphasis original.

78.   Uchitelskaya gazeta, 4 Mar. 1980.

79.   Filippov, 'Sotsiologicheskie problemy obrazovaniya v SSSR,' p. 20.

80.   Filippov, Sotsiologiya obrazovaniya, p. 99.

81.   Uchitelskaya gazeta, 2 Apr. 1977 and 24 June 1978. Paton is at pains to point out that he does not mean 'schools for gifted children' (i.e. presumably children who elsewhere might be deemed to be generally gifted) because of the unhealthy sense of exclusiveness bred in such places.

82.   E.G. Antosenkov, 'Different facets of the same problem,' Current Digest of the Soviet Press, vol. 29, no. 27 (1977), p. 9 (abstracted from Ekonomika i organizatsiya promyshlennovo proizvodstva, 1977, no. 3, pp. 96-105).

83.   I.S. Bolotin, 'Vozdeistvie demograficheskoi situatsii na srednyuyu i vysshuyu shkolu,' Sotsiologicheskie issledovaniya, 1979, no. 4, pp. 127-8.

84.   Ibid., Uchitelskaya gazeta, 25 June 1978.

85.   Antosenkov, 'Different facets of the same problem,' p. 9.

86.   Shvartsburd, 'Matematicheskaya spetsializatsiya,' p. 16.

87.   Hetsch, Uber Spezialklassen, pp. 22-5, quoting Shvartsburd.

88.   The phrase is the Ministry of Education's; the emphasis is mine.

89.   John Dunstan, 'Attitudes to provision for gifted children: the case of the USSR,' in Bruce M. Shore et al. (eds), Face to Face with Giftedness (Trillium Press, New York, 1983), pp. 290-327, at pp. 307-8.

90.   'Tesnee svyaz s zhiznyu, s praktikoi,' Narodnoe obrazovanie, 1983, no. 1, pp. 3-8, at p. 4; Literaturnaya gazeta, 19 Jan. 1983.

91.   'O vypolnenii plana razvitiya narodnovo obrazovaniya v 1982 godu i zadachakh na 1983 god v svete

reshenii noyabrskovo (1982 goda) Plenuma TsK KPSS,' BNA, 1983, no. 3, pp. 3-12, at p. 11.

92. Pravda, 4 Jan. 1984 (draft) and 14 Apr. 1984 (final text). Latter translated in Current Digest of the Soviet Press, vol. 36, no. 18 (1984), pp. 12-20.

93. Uchitelskaya gazeta, 16 June 1983.

94. Uchitelskaya gazeta, 16 July 1983.

95. Uchitelskaya gazeta, 29 Sep. 1983; Literaturnaya gazeta, 12 Oct. 1983.

96. Uchitelskaya gazeta, 1 Mar. 1984.

97. Uchitelskaya gazeta, 28 Feb. 1984.

98. E.g. Izvestiya, 30 Jan. 1984.

99. 'O tipovykh uchebnykh planakh dlya shkol (klassov) s uglublyennym teoreticheskim i prakticheskim izucheniem predmetov i s prepodavaniem ryada predmetov na inostrannom yazyke,' BNA, 1986, no. 2, pp. 14-21.

100. 'Tipovoe polozhenie o shkolakh (klassakh) s uglublyonnym teoreticheskim i prakticheskim izucheniem uchebnykh predmetov,' BNA, 1986, no. 5, pp. 42-4.

101. 'New model curriculum,' Soviet Education Study Bulletin, vol. 3, no. 2 (1985), pp. 65-7, citing BNA, 1985, no. 6, p. 24; 'O tipovykh uchebnykh planakh,' pp. 20-1.

102. 'O tipovykh uchebnykh planakh,' pp. 16-20.

103. Ibid., pp. 20-1; 'Ob uchebnykh planakh shkol s uglublyennym izucheniem ryada predmetov i s prepodavaniem ryada predmetov na inostrannykh yazykakh,' BNA, 1980 no. 4, pp. 23-37, at p. 37.

104. 'Ob uchebnykh planakh,' pp. 26-35; 'O tipovykh uchebnykh planakh,' pp. 16-20.

105. Uchitelskaya gazeta, 22 Aug. 1985.

106. Uchitelskaya gazeta, 27 Dec. 1984.

107. 'Plan-zakaz Ministerstva prosveshcheniya SSSR Akademii pedagogicheskikh nauk SSSR na razrabotku problem sovershenstvovaniya obucheniya i vospitaniya podrastayushchevo pokoleniya v 1986-1990 godakh,' BNA, 1986, no. 7, pp. 16-37, at p. 18.

108. 'Tipovoe polozhenie,' pp. 43-4.

109. 'On restructuring and the Party's cadre policy,' TASS text of Gorbachov's report at Plenum, 27 January 1987.

110. Galina Mylnikova, 'Falshivaya nota,' Sobesednik, 1986, no. 38, p. 10.

111. Sovetskaya Rossiya, 7 Feb. 1987; Moskovskaya pravda, 15 Feb. 1987.

112. M. Budanov, reported in TASS in Russian for

abroad, 31 Jan. 1987; Summary of World Broadcasts, SU/8484/B/5, 5 Feb. 1987.
113. Moskovskaya pravda, 15 Feb. 1987.
114. Sovetskaya Rossiya, 1 Mar. 1987.
115. 'Um die Aufnahme in die Spezialschulen,' Osteuropa, vol. 34, no. 11/12 (1984), pp. A630-1 (excerpts from Sovetskaya Litva, 15 February 1984).
116. Guardian, 13 Mar. 1982.
117. 'Um die Aufnahme,' p. A631.
118. Moskovskaya pravda, 15 Feb. 1987.
119. Sovetskaya Rossiya, 22 Feb. 1987.
120. Ibid.; Moskovskaya pravda, 15 Feb. and 10 Mar. 1987.
121. 'Tipovoe polozhenie,' p. 43.
122. Sovetskaya Rossiya, 7 Feb. 1987.
123. Moskovskaya pravda, 15 Feb. 1987.
124. Moskovskaya pravda, 10 Mar. 1987.
125. Sovetskaya Rossiya, 22 Feb. 1987.
126. Literaturnaya gazeta, 8 Apr. 1987.
127. Sovetskaya Rossiya, 22 Feb. 1987. See also letters in Sovetskaya Rossiya, 1 Mar. 1987.
128. Literaturnaya gazeta, 8 Apr. 1987.
129. Sovetskaya Rossiya, 22 Feb. 1987; 1968 data in Dunstan, Paths to Excellence, p. 94.
130. Sovetskaya Rossiya, 1 Mar. 1987; Moskovskaya pravda, 10 Mar. 1987.
131. Uchitelskaya gazeta, 23 Mar. 1985.
132. Moskovskaya pravda, 15 Feb. 1987.
133. Sovetskaya Rossiya, 7 Feb. 1987.
134. Sovetskaya Rossiya, 22 Feb. 1987.
135. Mylnikova, 'Falshivaya nota,' p. 10; 'Spetsshkola: yest problemy, net problem?,' Sobesednik, 1987, no. 5, p. 11.
136. Sovetskaya Rossiya, 7 Feb. 1987; Moskovskaya pravda, 15 Feb. and 10 Mar. 1987.
137. Spravochnik dlya postupayushchikh v vysshie uchebnye zavedeniya SSSR v 1983 godu (Vysshaya shkola, Moscow, 1983), pp. 184, 190, 201; ... v 1985 godu (Vysshaya shkola, Moscow, 1985), pp. 243, 258.
138. 'O tipovykh uchebnykh planakh,' pp. 14, 21.
139. Moskovskaya pravda, 15 Feb. 1987.
140. Sovetskaya Rossiya, 7 Feb. 1987.
141. Mylnikova, 'Falshivaya nota,' p. 10; ('Spetsshkola,' p. 11; Rostislav Devyataev, letter in Sobesednik, 1986, no. 41.

142. Sovetskaya Rossiya, 7 Feb. 1987; Moskovskaya pravda, 15 Feb. 1987.

143. '"U nas uzhe ne perekhodniy vozrast ...",' Yunost, 1982, no. 1, p. 81.

144. Moskovskaya pravda, 15 Feb. 1987.

145. Sovetskaya Rossiya, 7 Feb. 1987.

146. Sovetskaya Rossiya, 1 Mar. 1987.

147. For a detailed account, see Literaturnaya gazeta, 25 Jan. 1984.

148. '27th CPSU Congress: Gorbachov's Report (concluded),' Summary of World Broadcasts, SU/8194/C, 27 Feb. 1986, pp. 18, 40, 41, 42.

Chapter Three

SPECIAL EDUCATION FOR HANDICAPPED PUPILS

Andrew Sutton

INTRODUCTION

Soviet special education has a long (and tumultuous) history. In tsarist Russia such special provision was scarce, but there was an awareness of the problems posed by the education of the handicapped, and what little that was available was good. As a US author puts it,

> the programmes at the Queen of Heaven School for the retarded in Petersburg and the curricula and methods at leading schools for the blind and deaf in tsarist Russia were excellent for their time, commensurate with programmes in Western Europe and the United States, and compare favourably with programmes in use today. (1)

Yet the special education system developed upon this base has been little studied in the West. True, there have been various 'travellers tales', reports by Western professionals on study tours, but these have not produced an appreciation of the system as a whole. (2) At last, however, a small comparative literature is beginning to appear; (3) there is even controversy: Aubrey has soundly rebuked Holowinsky for his lack of a comparative approach. (4) But it will need incomparably greater attention before a full picture of the workings of this system becomes clearer and its promises and problems are fully revealed.

CHILD DEVELOPMENT AND DEFECTOLOGY

The system of special education in the Soviet Union is only comprehensible in the light of its underlying goals, both for the individuals involved and for special education as a whole. The two aspects are inextricably linked, both stemming from the common Marxist ideological notion of the perfectibility of humankind.

The conventional view of the origins of human intelligence and personality, which permeates and dominates Western educational provision, is that of dualism. Human mental development, according to this view, is a product of two factors: on the one hand, children's hereditary endowment, on the other, the effects of the environment in which children live. It is recognised that there may be some interaction between the two but the major question inevitably emerges: which of the two factors is primary in this interaction? The argument then rages between the 'hereditarians', who believe that documented differences in human attainment between different social classes, ethnic groups and sexes are the product of inherent biological differences, and the 'environmentalists', who assert that such differences are the product of the differing environments in which children grow. The former position is generally regarded as conservative in political terms, the latter radical. There are also more extreme positions which hold either that the differences are quite unimportant or that there are no differences at all.

The Soviet Marxist position was developed out of intense ideological struggle in the 1920s and early 1930s, and in the context of an economically backward and ethnically diverse state in the throws of rapid urbanisation and industrialisation. (5) It is founded directly upon Marx and Engels, but focuses upon ontogenesis, i.e. upon the history and development of each individual from birth in the wider context of historical materialism, with the dualism of heredity and environment overlaid by the introduction of a third factor, obuchenie, 'teaching'.

The Russian word obuchenie is a tricky one for English translators. It may be rendered by either 'teaching' or 'learning' and does indeed mean both; it refers to both aspects of these linked processes. Western psychology is a psychology of learning - and Western special education tends to deal with 'learning difficulties', i.e. problems inherent in the child. Early translators therefore used the word 'learning' unthinkingly. There is now consensus amongst Western scholars that the ideological base of Soviet psychology requires the translation 'teaching', so as to reflect the emphasis that child development is not a passive process in which the child merely learns and develops, but an active one in which adults teach and develop the child. This emphasis also grants that children do take an active role in their own learning and development and that ultimately, in adolescence, a 'fourth factor', young people assuming responsibility for the course of their own development, comes into play.

This dialectical and materialist understanding of child development has had to steer a sometimes awkward course between shifting ideological and practical demands, and it has never been a monolith. Nevertheless, the following extract fairly summarises the Zeitgeist into which the Soviet teacher-training system seeks to socialise student teachers with respect to the all-important relationship between teaching and development.

> Development is the process of the child's mastering socio-historical experience. The mind of humans and animals is in a state of continual development. The character and content of the processes of development in the animal world and in humans differ, however, qualitatively. The mental functions of humans and animals cannot be identified with each other in origin or in structure. The basic mechanism of the development of the mind of animals is the transmission of inherited, biologically consolidated experience. At its basis is the unfolding of the animal's developing adaptation to its external environment. The peculiar character of the mental functions of humans is that they develop in the process of the child's mastery of socio-historical experience. The child is born and lives in a human world, a world of human objects and human relationships, which contains the experience of social practice. The child's development is the process of mastering this experience. This process is realised in conditions of continual guidance by adults, i.e. in teaching (obuchenie).

> People's mental activity in its highest forms bears a mediated character. Already in antiquity people were using special objects, conditional representations and signs as a means of fixing and transmitting certain

information in the process of labour activity and teaching. Signs and speech mediate people's activity and the process of teaching. Consequently, the beginning and development of these means, including the development of culture, primarily defines the process of the historical development of the mind. It is the mastery of these means that is the process of individual development. The child masters the experience in human history. The child's thinking, memory and perception essentially develop by mastering speech, certain modes of activity and learning.

Over human history there have developed the means of accomplishing activity; but a <u>special way of transmitting these means, or social experience to successive generations</u> also took shape, developed and became more complicated. This specific way is <u>teaching</u>. It is the <u>unswerving and specially organised means of transmitting social experience. Thus, teaching plays a definite role in the process of the child's mental development.</u> (6)

The architect of this view, L.S. Vygotsky (1896-1934) was not only a psychologist and philosopher, he also worked clinically with backward children. In the process of working out his theory of mental development (which he termed 'cultural-historical'), he advanced an important new notion, central to Soviet understanding of what needs be done for backward or handicapped children, the zone of next development (ZND) (<u>zona blizhaishevo razvitiya</u> - sometimes also translated in the USA as 'zone of proximal development'). This is how Vygotsky explained his notion

Psychological research into the problem of teaching has usually been restricted to establishing a child's level of mental development. But it is not enough to define the state of a child's development by means of this level alone. How is this level usually defined? Problems that the child solves on his own serve as the means to define it. We will learn from these what the child can do and what he knows today, since we pay attention solely to the problems which the child can solve on his own. It is apparent that by this method we can only establish what has already matured within the child at the present day. We determine only the level of his present development. But the state of development is never defined only by that part of it which is already mature. Just as a gardener who wants to determine the state of his garden will be wrong if he takes it into his head to evaluate it solely on the basis of the apple trees which have ripened and are full of fruit, so too the psychologist, when he is evaluating the state of development, must inevitably take account not of the present level but also of the zone of next development. How is this to be done?

When we define the level of present development we use problems that require the child to solve them on his own and which are indicative only of functions that have already matured and taken shape. But let us try a new method. Let us suppose that we have determined the mental age of two children and that for both of them it is eight years. If we do not stop there, but try to show how both children solve problems which are meant for children of the next age level and which they are in no position to solve on their own, if help comes to them in the form of demonstration, a leading question, the start of the solution, etc, then it turns out that one of them, with help, with cooperation and under instruction, solves tasks up to the 12-year level, the other to the nine-year level. This discrepancy between the mental age, or the level of present development, which is determined by problems that the child has solved on his own, and the level of problem-solving that the child achieves when he is not working on his own but in cooperation, defines the zone of next development. In our example the zone of next development is defined by the figure 4 in the one child, by the figure 1 in the other.

Can we then consider that both children stand at an identical mental level, that the state of their development is the same? Clearly we cannot. As investigation shows, there prove to be far greater differences between these two children at school, caused by the discrepancy between their zones of next development, than there are similarities arising from the identical level of their present development. This shows above all in the dynamics of their mental development in the course of teaching and in their relative school achievement. Investigation shows that the zone of next development has more direct

significance for the dynamics of mental development
and school achievement than does the present level of
children's development. (7)

Vygotsky's ZND offers a dialectical approach to
assessing child development, regarding the individual child's
development as the current but dynamic product of two
processes, teaching and learning. Moreover, the dynamic of
development is one that proceeds through qualitative leaps,
a model that has profound implications for how one views
backwardness in children.

In recent years the British have learned to think in
terms of a 'continuum of need'; before that they have had a
long tradition, stretching back to the early work of Cyril
Burt, of thinking about mental backwardness as something
best described in terms of points upon a long, sweeping
curve that runs downwards from the lower limits of
normality right through to the most profound mental
incapacity. (8) At best, groups of children could be
distinguished as being placed within 'ranges' along this curve
(currently we speak of 'mild', 'moderate' and 'severe'
learning difficulties) but the boundaries of these ranges are
imprecise and we also speak of 'borderline cases'. It can
therefore be hard to grasp the Soviet model, which depends
on sharp qualitative distinctions, not just different levels of
backwardness but different kinds, with correspondingly
different educational requirements.

The most fundamental such distinction is between
oligophrenia (oligofreniya) and other forms of backwardness.

Oligophrenes (deti-oligofreny) are children whose
mental and academic retardation is caused by central
nervous system disorder of such a nature as to prevent their
learning and generalising as most children do. This
underlying disorder is irreversible and life-long and though,
as with all handicapped children, enormous progress can be
made with appropriate special-educational help, oligophrenia imposes limits that can never be wholly overcome.
Oligophrenes fall into three levels of severity. The largest
and least afflicted group are termed 'debiles' (deti-debily),
the more severely handicapped 'imbeciles' (imbetsily) and
the most profound 'idiots' (idioty). The differentiation
between levels of oligophrenia, and, most importantly,
between oligophrenia and other kinds of backwardness,
depends upon consideration of the child's ZND.

This careful differentiation of the minority group of

oligophrenes from amongst the wider population of the backward is an ideological necessity. It recognises that there is a small group of retarded children who have, to varying degrees, suffered damage to the material base, the central nervous system, so serious as to preclude the normal developmental mechanisms within the social interaction of adult and child. The corrolary to this is also ideologically based - and has profound practical implications. Children who are backward but <u>not</u> oligophrenic, as indicated by their ZND, <u>have normal potential whatever their current level of functioning</u> and it is the responsibility of society, acting primarily (though not solely) through its schools, to ensure that this potential is fulfilled.

As Vygotsky pointed out, two children might appear similarly backward in their development according to superficial aspects of what they can <u>currently</u> do. This is the fundamental Soviet objection to Western-style intelligence tests (one not generally advanced by their liberal critics). But the two children might prove fundamentally different when <u>taught</u>. The one might make only the smallest mechanical gains and prove unable to generalise what had been incorporated to new situations. The other might show rapid advances, once the principles of a task had been mastered, and go on to use such principles effectively in other, analogous situations. The former child, the oligophrene, will require slow, careful, methodical teaching, with plenty of practice, aiming only at limited academic skills. The latter will demand special compensatory measures, according to the underlying cause of the retardation, with a view ultimately of catching up and mastering the whole mass school curriculum. The underlying cause of the retardation in some such children will be physiologically-based temporary delays - in others no more than 'pedagogical neglect' (<u>pedagogicheskoe izvrashchenie</u>) on the part of either parents or teachers (see Chapter 6). It is now clear that the pedagogically neglected and the temporarily retarded are quite distinct categories.

Children with peripheral problems, such as disorders of speech, vision or learning, are similarly deemed to have normal potential (granting that they do not also suffer from a complicating oligophrenia) and their educational requirements will be compensatory measures to enable them to master the mass school curriculum.

Curricular goals and educational provision

The Soviet education service is typically described as providing special schools for specific categories of pupils, the deaf, the hard-of-hearing, the blind, the weak-sighted, those with problems of speech or problems of movement. There are also schools for those whom we in the United Kingdom term 'delicate' and schools for children with temporary delays in mental development. By far the largest category are the 'auxiliary' (vspomogatelnye) schools, for oligophrenes of the debile grade. (9) In practice, there is considerable local diversity and the range of schools provided can be extensive. The special-school provision in the Armenian Republic, as described to myself by local Ministry of Education (Minpros) officials in 1986, is outlined in Table 3.1. (10) Surprising is the high level of provision of a sort that we would call 'delicate': seven convalescent schools (including a forest sanitorium) and specialist schools for scoliosis (bent spine) and cardiac-rheumatic cases. Either the system makes special placements at the slightest hint of an enfeebled physical condition, or Armenia has a relatively high level of children in rather poor physical condition.

Table 3.1: Special schools for handicapped (anomalnye) children in Armenia (October 1986)

Deaf	1
Hard-of-hearing	1
Blind	1
Weak-sighted	5
Problems of movement	1
Problems of speech	3
Temporary delay in development	3
Scoliosis	1
Heart conditions and rheumatism	1
Convalescent (including in a forest sanatorium)	7
Behaviour problems	1
Nervous	1
Debile (auxiliary schools)	17
Total	43

Source: personal communication in Yerevan, Armenia

Except in the case of auxiliary schools, the goal of special schools (most of which are at least partially residential) is to teach the normal mass-school curriculum. This will require combinations of special methods, ancillary paramedical staff, smaller classes, specially trained teachers and care staff, and extra years to master the curriculum. The goal, however separate and different these schools may be from the mainstream of ordinary family and social life, is to teach the same basic skills, knowledge and attitudes as inculcated in every Soviet child. The major exception is the auxiliary school, which aims at teaching only the elementary grades over the total period of schooling. As I observed on my visit to Armenia in 1986, a school for children with movement problems may run two parallel streams, one for motor-disordered children capable of following the normal mass-school curriculum, the other for those who are doubly handicapped, both motor-disordered and oligophrenic, for whom the auxiliary curriculum is provided.

These curricular goals of the special-education system fit closely the theoretical understanding of child development already outlined: as long as the actual cortical basis for thinking and learning remains intact, then children, whatever their problems, have the same potential as do any others.

Outside Minpros

The system provides clear limits for what is possible in curricular terms. Oligophrenic children of the debile grade are capable of mastering the lower reaches of the academic syllabus, and are educated accordingly. Some children, however, are not deemed capable of participating profitably in this way - and therefore do not come under the aegis of Minpros at all. Children with a more severe mental handicap (the deti-imbetsily) do not attend a school but an 'establishment' (uchrezhdenie) or a 'children's home' (detsky dom) run by the Ministries of Social Security. Here they are taught by teachers provided by Minpros, but the syllabus is non-academic, focusing upon basic personal, social, self-help and occupational skills. Another group excluded from the Minpros special-school are children with physical or multiple disabilities - particularly, it appears from personal enquiries, children with more severe problems of movement or continence. This is a major practical divergence between Soviet and much Western provision. Children in Minpros schools for movement problems suffer from far less severe physical complaints than would be found in British schools for the physically handicapped. In the Soviet school the children would all be mobile and able to use their hands for ordinary curricular activities, while in the British many of the pupils would be wheelchair-bound or only able to use their hands effectively with the aid of special apparatus. A proportion of the British pupils would be incontinent. In the Soviet Union, immobile, non-dextrous, incontinent children are catered for outside the Minpros special-school system, either by means of home tuition or under the Ministry of Social Security. There is one further group excluded from Minpros schools: deti-idioty and 'psychiatric' cases (e.g. autistic or psychotic children) fall outside Minpros and are either cared for by the Ministry of Health or left in the care of their families.

Thus the social role of the Minpros special-education system is not to provide education for all, however handicapped, adapted to the needs of the individual child, however deviant or limited. Rather it is to provide a common training, education and socialisation to everyone in the younger generation who could conceivably benefit, leaving the residuum to be catered for elsewhere. This 'elsewhere' should not be thought of as necessarily inferior or second-rate: the deaf-blind children's home at Zagorsk is precisely one of these non-Minpros establishments, and may be fairly regarded as one of the heights of special-educational practice anywhere in the world (see Chapter 5).

TRAINING AND RESEARCH

The teachers in Minpros schools are called 'defectologists' (defektologi), and have a five-year initial training in teaching handicapped children. Defectologists are paid 20% more than teachers in the mass schools, like whom they must attend a refresher course every five years or lose their licence to teach. Their basic training is carried out at the defectological faculties of pedagogical institutes. There are now 15 such faculties in the USSR, the largest of which, at the Lenin Pedagogical Institute in Moscow, has over 1100 students from all over the USSR, plus about 100 teachers annually on in-service courses to retrain as defectologists.

There are also around 80 foreign students from socialist countries and the Third World.

The staff of special schools also include vospitateli (child-care staff, or 'upbringers'), responsible for children's non-academic activities. These are also required to have specialised defectological training.

The staffing complement at each school varies according to the nature of school and the handicap provided for. For example, in 1986, Auxiliary School No. 530 in Moscow accommodated 396 day children in 23 classes. The staff of the school comprised 38 defectologists, five upbringers, one psychoneurologist (a physician specialising in childhood developmental disorders, one nurse and a logoped (similar to a speech therapist). A hundred of the children stayed on after school hours until around six p.m. for activities which included supervised homework, during which time they were under the supervision of the five upbringers. This may be contrasted with the school for children with motor problems in Yerevan, the capital of Armenia, with 142 pupils, 80 of them residential. Only ambulent and continent children were accepted, all but 26 of whom were suffering from light forms of cerebral palsy. Eight of the school's classes (59 children) followed the normal mass-school curriculum, 15 (81 children) the curriculum for auxiliary schools. This school had 47 defectologists and 22 upbringers. Also employed full-time in situ as an integral part of the school's staff (i.e. not just as visiting specialists) was a 'medical cabinet' of 22: six doctors of various specialisms, 4 logopeds, plus nursing staff and LFKs (staff providing lechebnaya fizkultura, or 'physiotherapy'). As an additional para-medical/social provision, sanatorium placement was available during vacations.

By British standards, then, both quantitatively and qualitatively, the level of professional provision in the special schools is high, even in far-away Armenia.

The Russian term defektologiya ('defectology') has no direct equivalent in English, referring to study of the laws of development, the upbringing and education of children with physical and mental inadequacies. It includes relevant branches of medicine and psychology, as well as pedagogy. The chief research establishment in this field is the Research Institute of Defectology of the USSR Academy of Sciences (NIID APN). This major establishment employs 140 research workers and 200 auxiliary staff, including psychologists, defectologists, logopeds, doctors of various specialisms and technicians. It studies the development of handicapped children and, in particular, ways of identifying specific subgroups, in order to generate new diagnostic, educational and compensatory approaches. It prepares text books and teachers' manuals, and organises in-service education. The <u>NIID</u> also publishes the journal <u>Defektologiya</u>. This is a substantial academic serial publication, appearing every two months, amounting to almost a hundred pages of closely printed text per issue, with a regular print-run of 45,000. Again by British standards, the system's infrastructure in terms of academic back-up is an impressive one. The term 'academic' is not used here in any perjorative sense: this is practical research, often carried out in real schools with its results having real effects upon practice. As Stringer writes:

> The Institute of Defectology advises the Ministry of Education on changes in special education. If these changes are accepted they become policy throughout the Soviet Union, amended as appropriate to local conditions. Apart from Institute-initiated research, there are also occasions when research is directly requested by the Ministry.
> All Union Republics have a Research Institute of Psychology and Pedgagogics, to which are attached 'laboratories' for studying handicaps. The Institute of Defectology has contact with all these laboratories, usually through individual research workers. When a particular piece of research is carried out at the Institute, efforts are made to conduct it in different regions of the Soviet Union. One example of this is the experiment designed to reduce the period of education deaf children need to complete their curriculum. Another example concerns the preparation for work of mentally retarded youngsters, where valuable research was undertaken in the Moldavian capital, Kishinyov. (11)

This is a well-established way of effecting educational change in the USSR. On a recent visit to Armenia I heard of an experimental class for imbecile children being run in an auxiliary school in Yerevan. In the city of Kirovakan I asked the head of a local auxiliary school what he thought of this experiment. Would he like such children in his own school? 'It's not a question of whether I'd like it or not,' he replied.

'If the experiment shows that it's better for the children, then of course we'll do it - and if it shows that it doesn't, then we won't.'

For all this provision and the attempt to found the work on a developing scientific base, what of the school children themselves? Stringer summarised his extensive, published field-work notes in a manner typical of reports by non-Soviet commentators:

As for children, I had been forewarned about their regimentation and lack of spontaneity, but my first experience of a break-time in school was a revelation, since there appeared to be unrestrained chaos! It was to be similar in all the schools I visited: children running in corridors (and being asked not to!), shouting, laughing, joking (so far as I could tell), being curious about my presence ... in other words very little different from children anywhere. I saw toys and games in abundance and no lack of opportunity for what we might term free-play. The children I saw at play in Moscow neighbourhoods, too, were recognisable as the children I see at play around my home in this country. (12)

PROBLEMS OF PROVISION

The formal and theoretical base of Soviet special education may well include advances (perhaps substantial ones) over what we know in the West. The elegant position on child development and its anomalies that have stemmed from the work of Vygotsky and his successors, rigorously applied across different disciplines and categories of provision, may well from its very consistency bring advantages over the pluralistic and eclectic systems more typical in the West. Substantially, too, the theory itself includes fundamental insights (ZND, for example) that have been eagerly taken up in recent years by more 'advanced' developmental psychologists in the West. For their own part, Soviet researchers are pleased to draw upon the (largely American) body of experimental data built up in the West to support their own general special-educational position. There has been little reciprocal traffic, however, in either ideas or experience to enrich Western special education - to our undoubted impoverishment.

Yet, whatever the heights of Soviet defectology, there

can be no doubt that the practical application of the system is not without its problems, and there are some indications where some at least of such problems may be found.

Regional variations

Anderson et al have made a most detailed examination of available Soviet statistical data to form a first, quantitative picture of childhood disability and special educational provision in the USSR. (13) A major shortcoming in this study comes from the authors' inability to trace any figures on children catered for outside Minpros special schools (i.e. under the Ministries of Health and of Social Security) and the subsequent necessity to rely upon figures for school placement, a secondary phenomenon, rather than upon the primary phenomenon of disability itself. This might be a very important issue in judging the effectiveness of the system as a whole for, if it should prove the case that substantial numbers of children are being excluded from the Minpros special-education system, then the apparent high achievements of that system could be in part explicable by its selectivity - an interesting paradox in a socialist state!

Notwithstanding, Anderson and her colleagues have presented a most detailed analysis of Minpros special education. Table 3.2 summarises some of their findings. The system has grown enormously in scale in the years following 1945, the increase having been particularly steep over the sixties and seventies. The rate of increase (both in absolute terms and proportionally) has been particularly high in some of the non-Russian regions, though with rather different effects in different regions.

In Transcaucasia and Central Asia the numbers of special-school pupils expanded from a very small base (respectively seven-fold and almost twelve-fold), though they are not altogether keeping pace with a fast rising school-age population, so that the overall population of pupils in special schools still remains around half that of the USSR as a whole. At the opposite end of the country, however, in the Baltic Republics, a four-fold increase in numbers has led to an astonishingly high population of pupils in special schools, nearly six per cent in the primary years. There seems no a priori reason to suspect that these major regional differences reflect differing prevalances of handicap across the regions of the USSR (indeed, one might

Table 3.2: Pupils in special schools, expressed in thousands, as a percentage of total school population in classes I-IV (ages 7 - 10) and in terms of overall increase 1960-1980

| | N(K) | | | % | | |
	1960	1980	Increase	1960	1980	Increase
Russian Republic	93	295	3.17	0.88	3.65	4.15
Ukraine, Belorussia and Moldavia	29	101	3.44	0.71	2.57	3.62
Baltic Republics (1)	6	27	4.40	1.39	5.82	4.19
Transcaucasian Republics (2)	2	17	7.18	0.25	1.34	5.36
Central Asian Republics (3)	5	60	11.78	0.20	1.34	6.70
Total USSR	135	500	3.68	7.30	2.73	3.74

(1) Latvia, Lithuania and Estonia
(2) Georgia, Armenia and Azerbaidzhan
(3) Uzbekistan, Kirgizia, Turkmenia, Tadzhikistan and Kazakhstan

Source: adapted from B.A. Anderson, B.D. Silver, V.A. Volkoff, 'Education of the handicapped in the USSR: exploration of the statistical picture,' Soviet Studies, vol. 39 (1987), pp. 468-88.

speculate a contrary gradient in favour of the more socially and economically advantaged regions). Instead, Anderson and her colleagues propose four possible social and economic explanations that appear plausibly to account for this considerable disproportion of provision.

Firstly, handicap may be differentially identified. Thus, where the preschool network is underdeveloped (as in Central Asia and in rural areas generally) early identification of handicap will be less likely. The same areas are also likely to fall short of approved quotas of doctors and other medical personnel. Further, it has to be remembered that the ordinary mass-school system has been only fully developed relatively recently in some Republics, matriculation in primary schools not being complete everywhere until the late 1950s. Secondly, the possibility exists of differential selection criteria in different regions - even if all potential candidates were to be brought forward by health and education agencies. This could be a factor not only of local professional and administrative practices, but also of differing cultural attitudes towards special-school placement. Thirdly, there is the degree of which it has yet proved possible to provide a properly elaborated special-educational network to meet complex local conditions. An important factor here is the problem of linguistic diversity, which will be dealt with in more detail below. Fourthly, republican budgets have to be considered. Despite central guidelines for funding republican school systems, there is room for local discretion on precise allocations. The high per capita cost of special school provision may make this area a vulnerable budget priority, particularly where a high rate of population growth puts strains upon the provision of ordinary mass schooling and the programmes of school building and staff training required to meet this wider demand.

Linguistic diversity

The USSR is a multi-lingual state. Russian is the official language of the USSR and the lingua franca, but more than half the schoolchildren in the country are not Russians. And because the Republics themselves are so diverse, for many pupils even the titular language of their Republic is not their first language. Few Russians are bilingual, but for non-Russian schoolchildren a policy of 'two streams' means that they have to learn to speak and study in Russian as well as in their native tongue - and for some the process of Russification means that Russian will be the prime medium of education.

Handicap and ethnicity in education bring together two already complex issues to create a labyrinthine puzzle for providers and consumers alike. For example, what language does one teach the young deaf child, the language of the state or of the family? If the answer is the latter (and this is a big 'if'), are there suitable materials available in, say, Uzbek, Armenian or Estonian? How does one give speech therapy to a young speech-impaired Volga German or Udmurt? How does one teach Braille to a blind Turkmenian, and will there then be Braille textbooks for this child to read in the higher grade levels? Are there appropriate curricular materials available for the Belorussian oligophrene?

Anderson and her colleagues have made a statistical analysis of the textbooks published for use in special schools over the years 1951-1981. Of the 15 titular republican languages,

> no textbooks for children with any kind of handicap were published in Belorussian, Kazakh, Kirghiz or Turkmenian in any year between 1951 and 1981. During the same period the first text in Tadzhik for handicapped children (for use in auxiliary schools) was published only in 1981. No textbook was published for handicapped children in the language of any other Soviet nationality during those years, including nationalities with sizeable populations, such as the Tatars. (14)

The authors do point out that lack of textbooks is at best only a crude index of provision and that, over the period in question guides for teachers and supplementary materials were published in Belorussian, Kazakh, Turkmenian and Tatar. Nevertheless, their data indicate considerable differences between categories of handicap and between the languages in which textbooks have been produced. Textbooks for the deaf have been published for years and are the more widely available, closely followed by those for auxiliary schools. And it is in the European part of the USSR that specialised textbooks have been longest available, in a wider range of languages, with Transcaucasia lagging behind somewhat and Central Asia more so. Only in Uzbek does the situation come close to that of the European part of the USSR, but even here not in the higher grade levels.

In the absence of textbooks that are appropriate to the child's handicap and written in a local language, special schools have to make recourse to two other kinds of material: either they must use textbooks designed for the mass school or fall back on materials in another language (probably Russian).

In Armenia in 1986 it was reported that one of the

auxiliary schools in the capital, Yerevan, included five classes specifically for Russian speakers. This is consistent with the situation in the mass schools in the Republic where, though Armenian children have to learn Russian, Russian children only take Armenian as an option. There are, however, no such special classes for handicapped children from the Georgian or Azerbaidzhan minorities within the republic, nor, apparently, for handicapped children in the Armenian communities elsewhere in the USSR.

Poor practice

The intense Soviet interest in careful differentiation, expressed both at the Research Institute for Defectology in Moscow and the directives from <u>Minpros</u>, is not always reflected in the day-to-day work of the system. Teachers in the mass schools may well put pressure on the special-school system to unload their more troublesome pupils, irrespective of whether or not they are really oligophrenes. As Novikov has written:

> On inspection of the auxiliary schools in the Chelyabinsk region (Urals) and Tula (Central Russia), the regional school authorities were censured by the Ministry because children were often sent to auxiliary schools on a diagnosis that did not conform to the formal instructions for acceptance into these institutions. In this ministerial decree there was also the criticism that decisions, which were all-important for the children, were taken without proper medical investigation. Apparently, some teachers in the ordinary schools had declared young misfits to be 'mentally handicapped' in the primary and also the secondary stage and had taken 'all possible measures to transfer such children to auxiliary schools'. (5)

Official sources are well aware of failures of implementation at all levels of the system, and satisfaction at achievement is tempered by admonitions for failure. Reviewing progress in the training of defectologists under the eleventh five-year plan (1981-1985), the leading article in a recent issue of <u>Defektologiya</u> was able to cite considerable quantitative progress: 18 faculties of defectology now in operation, including new ones opened in

Kazakhstan, Kirgizia and the Mordovian Autonomous Republic, 14,000 young specialists having graduated over the last five years. But, quoting Gorbachov, the authors pointed sternly to the need for improving the <u>quality</u> of work in these defectological faculties:

> To a significant degree, since 1970 the publication plans for textbooks on defectology for students in education institutions have not been met. In 1981-1985 the following materials were not produced: <u>The History of Logopedics</u>, <u>Teaching the Deaf</u> (in two volumes), <u>Fundamentals of Defectology</u>, <u>Oligophrenopedagogy</u> and others.
> What are the reasons? Firstly, having taken upon themselves the responsibility of preparing material, certain authors for whatever reasons could not write them. Secondly, the Scientific-Method Council on Defectology at the USSR Ministry of Education has not displayed due persistence in organising and controlling authors' work. And thirdly (evidently one of the chief reasons) the editorial board of the publishing house <u>Prosveshchenie</u> has not shown due activity in this process. (16)

THE CONSUMERS' VOICE

The lot of the adult disabled in the USSR has been the subject of sparse but widely contradictory accounts. On the one hand are official or quasi-official accounts. For example, Gitlits, a Soviet journalist, has recently published for foreign consumption a collection of cameos based upon interviews with a number of disabled Soviet people. (17) His reports catalogue some truly remarkable human achievements, not just by the disabled themselves but also by those who work and live with them, all within the context of a benevolent and caring state. On the other hand, there are reports from <u>emigre</u> disabled dissidents that paint a grim picture of neglect by the social agencies, with outright oppression by the KGB and psychiatric services if one dares to complain. (18) Whatever the overall picture, the USSR appears to offer very wide extremes of the experience of disability.

At the younger age range, whilst the USSR clearly provides some exceptional help for handicapped children and their families, perhaps not all parents are altogether happy with how services are arranged. Even in Gitlits' book one glimpses parents' dilemma at having to send their handicapped children to a special school often situated a considerable distance from home. Parents do have a choice but it tends to be Hobson's! There is no legal basis for the authorities to insist that a child should receive education in a special school rather than in the mass school. If parents do not agree to special-school placement then the choice is that they, the child and the teachers in the mass school will have to manage as well as they can - or that the child drops out of school altogether, perhaps with a visiting home teacher. In practice, most parents evidently take the special school - or, as was reported to me by one official in 1986, they struggle along on their own, then change their decision when the case is reviewed a year later.

Izvestiya has recently published a long letter of complaint by a mother whose second daughter lost her hearing following an infection. The family was faced with a bald choice: either placement in a boarding school in Khabarovsk (over thirteen hundred miles away) for the rest of her childhood or the whole family tackling her education and upbringing at home. This family chose the latter course and found it a tough one, not just in itself but all the more so because of the response of professionals and authorities generally. The letter said:

> In no way do I want to judge those who exercise their right to put their child in the care of the state. The parents can go on as they did before, raise their other children and work and live, while the sick child is cared for, fed, looked after and educated, as far as that is possible. But isn't enormous respect due to those fathers and mothers, brothers, sisters, grandmothers and grandfathers who, no matter what condition the child was born in, want it to grow up in the family?
>
> Meanwhile, look at the injustice, unwarranted insults, reproaches, misunderstandings and even outright hostility that are sometimes encountered by the family that has made this choice. In a recent article in a special journal for teachers, the author (an Academician) stated that 'examples of this kind are hardly deserving of imitation.' Imagine saying something like that! True, it was a journal article. But what of the institutions that we and others like us

appeal to for basic assistance, which is often quite easy to provide?

First and foremost, every family of this kind must know where to turn if it is in trouble and must feel confident that it will receive help. We rushed around looking for help without success ... Our explanations and the very fact that we wanted to keep our child at home were treated by everyone as mere caprice. What wasn't I accused of, when I should have been getting sympathy! (19)

The family soldiered on, suffering particularly from an inflexible system of disability pensions until normalisation was achieved: 'Yes, she was once disabled, but the reason we worked by the sweat of our brow for all these years was so that now she can go to school right here in the neighbourhood, just like any other child.'

The official attitude shares Mrs Yatsunova's goals but takes issue with the integrationist position current in the West, that handicapped children are best educated amongst their non-handicapped peers.

In Soviet defectology integration is regarded as the ultimate purpose of education in that anyone from a special school must enter society as a full member, capable of living independently, of interacting with the people around him and of engaging in productive activity ...

Experience in developing the system of special education in the USSR has shown that the most effective way of preparing handicapped children for integration into society is instruction in special schools. We contrast this approach with the mechanical (i.e. mechanistic - AS) solution whereby the handicapped child is placed in an ordinary class among normally developing children of the same age and given the option of some brief additional coaching by a teacher specializing in work with people with the defect in question ...

Such mechanical (mechanistic) integration is always associated with a lowering of demands made of the handicapped child, so that he ultimately falls short of normally developing children in terms of knowledge and skills. (20)

Of necessity, Yatsunova's experience was not one of 'mechanical integration' straight into the local mass school (this appears not to have been on offer). Instead, she steered a difficult middle way. Perhaps other parents are making their wishes felt, so as to affect wider policy. It was suggested to me in Moscow in 1986, by the head of a highly acclaimed school for the temporarily retarded, that the introduction of special classes in mass schools was, in part at least, a response to parents' reluctance to send their mildly affected children away to a boarding school, however excellent, such as his.

The slowly emerging picture of Soviet special education is still sparse and its general impression contradictory. Some clarity may derive from distinguishing between two levels of the system - on the one hand, the psychopedagogical and pedagogic, on the other, the social and economic. Many visitors and writers have tended to confound the two, often grossly misunderstanding fundamental aspects of the former and permitting their political views on the Soviet Union to tinge their observations on the latter.

But this is a developing field and sounder analyses are emerging which suggest that in both areas, psychopedagogical and sociological, there is great diversity. Soviet defectology works on most sophisticated philosophical and psychological theory, it has highly developed techniques and has demonstrated the most exceptional pedagogy. The organisation and provision of the system of special education and its infrastructure are truly remarkable. My own observations in Armenia suggest that such heights of achievement are not restricted to the major research institutes or the metropolitan centres of the European part of the USSR. On the other hand, there are difficulties. Exciting theoretical frameworks often have little experimental confirmation, there are problems of maintaining standards across the system (standards of professional thinking as well as practice), and of provision across a huge, diverse, expanding and still economically weak society.

Further, from the point of view of the Westerner, the system can seem fairly inflexible, in both its psychopedagogic and sociological manifestations. But Westerners who criticise it on these terms must take care to guard against careless and ethnocentric thinking that takes their own situation or ideology as the unproblematical benchmarks against which all others should be measured. It is easy for Western professionals (especially Anglo-Americans) to shy away from a uniform theoretical system with an explicit philosophical base, but they usually do so from a personal stance founded upon eclecticism and empiricism that may find the Soviet position profoundly unsettling. And it can be all too easy to wax pious about Soviet attitudes to parental choice and integration, but one does so from a society in which pressure-group politics are a normal, legitimate and lauded feature of our national life. In the Soviet Union things are rather different and it is the education system and its political masters that determine its own shape (not so very different than was the case in the West not so long ago).

If one does feel obliged to make judgements about the achievements (or otherwise) of Soviet special education for handicapped children, then it is well to remember that the situation over there, like here, is dynamic and developing under the impetus of real social forces, and that the problems encountered should not be solely constructed as specifically Soviet - or even Russian, Armenian, Estonian, Ukrainian, Uzbek, or whatever. There may be common issues of conceptualisation and social response raised wherever an advanced economy faces up to the problems of providing education for all children. The problems outlined here - of regional inequality, equitable provision for ethnic minorities, the maintenance of high quality practice and the proper representation of parental views - are hardly areas in which Western societies can claim unqualified success. Despite all their obvious differences, Soviet and Western special educators may in fact have more in common than that which divides them.

NOTES

1.   M.S. Conroy, 'Education of the blind, deaf and mentally retarded in tsarist Russia,' Slavic and European Education Review, vols. 1 and 2 (1985), pp. 29-30.

2.   A. Sutton, 'Review essay,' Slavic and European Education Review, vols. 1 and 2 (1985), pp. 89-94.

3.   See A. Sutton, 'Backward children in the USSR,' in M. Perrie, J. Brine and A. Sutton (eds.), Home, School and Leisure in the Soviet Union (Allen and Unwin, London, 1980), pp. 160-191; L. Novikov, 'Some aspects of the development

of special education in the Soviet Union,' in J. Tomiak (ed.), Western Perspectives on Soviet Education in the 1980s (Macmillan, London, 1986), pp. 191-207; B.A. Anderson, B.D. Silver, V.A. Volkoff, 'Education of the handicapped in the USSR: exploration of the statistical picture,' Soviet Studies, vol. 39 (1987), pp. 468-88.

4.　　See C. Aubrey, 'A response to "School psychology in the USA and USSR",' School Psychology International, vol. 8 (1987), pp. 173-5; I.Z. Holowinsky, 'School psychology in the USA and USSR: a brief comparison,' School Psychology International, vol. 7 (1986), pp. 35-9.

5.　　R.A. Bauer, The New Man in Soviet Psychology (University of Wisconsin Press, Madison, 1952).

6.　　A.V. Petrovsky, Vozrastnaya i pedagogicheskaya psikhologiya (Prosveshchenie, Moscow, 1973), pp. 21-2.

7.　　L.S. Vygotsky, Sobranie sochinenii (Pedagogika, Moscow, 1982), vol. 2, pp. 246-7.

8.　　See A. Sutton, 'L.S. Vygotsky: the cultural-historical theory, national minorities and the zone of next development,' in R. Gupta and P. Coxhead (eds), Cultural Diversity and Learning Efficiency: Recent Developments in Assessment (Macmillan, London, 1988), pp. 89-117.

9.　　See A.I. Dyachkov, Defektologichesky slovar, Second edition (Prosveshchenie, Moscow, 1970).

10.　　Western visitors to Soviet special schools usually follow a well-beaten track to by now well-reported Moscow and Leningrad institutions, which are doubtless excellent examples of special pedagogy in action. The present author's visit to Armenia provided an opportunity to see some schools not previously visited by Westerners. There seems no reason to consider the schools seen in this Transcaucasian Republic as in any way show-places. See A. Suddaby and A. Sutton, 'Special education for handicapped children in the Armenian Republic,' Soviet Education Study Bulletin, Summer, 1988.

11.　　P. Stringer, 'Special education in the Soviet Union and the child with learning difficulties,' Journal of the Association of Educational Psychologists, vol. 6, no. 4 (1984), pp.2-3.

12.　　Ibid., p. 7.

13.　　B.A. Anderson et al, 'Education of the handicapped.'

14.　　Ibid., p. 471.

15.　　L. Novikov, 'Some aspects of the development of special education,' p. 200.

16. Yu. G. Kruglov and N.P. Pivovarova, 'Problemy podgotovki uchitelei-pedagogov v pedagogicheskikh institutakh,' Defektologiya, vol. 1 (1986), p. 7.

17. I. Gitlits, Leading a Full Life Regardless (Novosti Press Agency, Moscow, 1984).

18. V. Fefilov, 'After 60 years of Soviet power, how humane is "developed socialism"?' Spastics News, 5 February 1984.

19. O. Yatsunova, Letter to Izvestiya, 15 April 1986.

20. V.I. Lyubovsky, 'Basic principles of special education in the USSR,' Prospects, vol. 11 (1981), p. 445.

Chapter Four

GIFTEDNESS IN SPORT

Jim Riordan

INTRODUCTION

Of all the disciplines accorded special education for the gifted, sport is the most outstanding. Not only does it possess the largest number of residential and special day schools, it has the most developed system of talent identification, testing and nurturing that far surpasses anything devoted to ballet, music, art or the sciences.

This high status for sports excellence is paralleled in several other socialist states, most notably the German Democratic Republic, China and Cuba. Further, it is a bias that finds no equivalent in the West, where special education in ballet and music, for example, is generally more widespread than that in sport.

While Soviet concern with talent in sport has a fairly long history, the promotion of boarding schools for gifted young athletes is relatively recent, dating from the late 1960s; it postdates by several decades the establishment of boarding schools for the cultivation of talent in ballet, music and art. Moreover, unlike ballet and music residential schools, the sports schools have no history in pre-revolutionary times.

The rapid expansion of such sports schools in the late 1970s and early 1980s has nonetheless come in for considerable criticism: of 'hot-house' athletes, of their privileges and precocious one-sided education, of the imbalance between resources allocated to elite sport, on the one hand, and 'sport for all', on the other. As in regard to excellence in other spheres, the debate currently underway is calling into question the ways that talent in sport is nurtured and rewarded in a socialist society.

To understand the debate and the attention given to sports excellence in Soviet society we have to examine the historical traditions, ideology and political priorities that have shaped official attitudes to sport and sports excellence in the USSR.

Historical and ideological background

In 1917 the new Soviet leadership inherited from tsarist Russia an incipient sports movement that differed in a number of ways from that which had developed in the West.

In Britain particularly, individual enthusiasts from among the leisured class had pioneered the development of certain organised sports, had given them their rules and conventions and often made them exclusive to their social, racial and sexual group. There were thus established single-sport clubs (eg for tennis, golf, soccer), governing bodies for individual sports separate from one another and from government, based for purposes of control and largely finance on their members. These voluntary, independent organisations therefore belonged to a particular social group with a particular social outlook, encapsulated in the concept of amateur-elitism. This quasi-aristocratic ethos tended to regard sport as the 'garden of human activities' (and a private garden at that), a leisure activity in which playing, not winning, was paramount, an activity unworthy of a career or remuneration, of professional coaches and centres of sporting excellence.

In Russia, on the other hand, as in the economy, the tsarist state had to some extent discouraged individual enterprise: it had established some control over the organisation of sport - in schools, the armed forces, the national federations and the Olympic Committee (Russia being a founder member of the International Olympic Committee). It had set up the Office of the Chief Supervisor of Sport headed by an army officer, General Voyeikov, to coordinate the sports movement. Moreover, most Russian clubs became multi-sport centres, in so far as the organisation of Russian sport had tended to develop in close association with the Olympic model; and these sports complexes were linked to local and central government, thereby enabling the tsarist regime to keep close supervision over the development of organised sport and to prevent it from being used for anti-monarchist, liberal or revolutionary purposes (as the Turner movement in Germany and the Sokol movement in the Czech lands had been).

The new Soviet government in 1917 was therefore able to take over a ready-made state organisation of sport without having to dismantle a wide-ranging structure of autonomous sports clubs and federations or to counter any firmly-rooted amateur values. What is more, with the sweeping away of a leisure class, there was no coherent group left in Soviet society to develop sport for its own disport.

A further vital influence on the Bolsheviks in their perception of sport was the ideological legacy they had received not only from Western social thinkers like Marx, Engels and Rousseau, but from progressive Russian social reformers like Chernyshevsky, Dobrolyubov, Tolstoy, Lesgaft and Pavlov - not forgetting Lenin. It has to be remembered that in much 19th century social thought metaphysics was in the grip of a dualism that separated mind from matter and, under the influence of Christian theology, often exaggerated a distinction into an antagonism; in such a world view, body and soul were seen as warring parties with the body cast as villain.

The progressive social thinkers rejected the dualist philosophy and stressed that not only was there an intimate relationship between matter and mind, but that the former largely determined the latter. In Marx's view, political and social institutions and the ideas, images and ideologies through which human beings understand the world in which they live, their place within it and themselves, ultimately derived from the economic base of society. This defined the class relations into which people had to enter with one another in order to produce:

> In the social production which people carry on they enter into certain relations that are indispensible and independent of their wills; these relations of production correspond to a certain stage of development of their material powers of production. The sum total of these relations of production constitutes the economic structure of society - the real foundation on which rise legal and political superstructures and to which correspond certain forms of social consciousness. The mode of production in material life determines the general nature of the social, political and spiritual

processes of life. It is not people's consciousness that determines their existence; on the contrary, it is their social existence that determines their consciousness. (1)

This is certainly not to deny inherited characteristics, but it does put the onus on the social environment for the way we think and express our various talents. It therefore contains certain implications for sport and physical exercise generally.

1.   Since the human psychosomatic organism develops and changes under the impact of external conditions, including the social environment, subjection to physical exercise not only develops that part of the body to which it is directed, but it also has an effect on the body as a whole - on the personality. A strong bond exists between social and individual development and between the physical and mental development of the individual. Societies are likely to seek to shape that development.

2.   In liberal capitalist society, whose prevailing ideology is that of 'independent' decision-making and 'free' contracting between 'equal' social atoms, sport has normally been regarded as the concern only of the individual, a feature of life unconnected with classes and social values, with society's mode of production; scant attention has traditionally been paid to it as a social phenomenon. To the Marxist, however, sport is part of the social superstructure and therefore strongly affected by the prevailing relations of production - not something 'in itself' and so divorced from politics; a society's pattern of sport will ultimately depend on the specifics of that society's socio-economic foundation, its class relationships. Moreover, says Marx, 'with a change in the economic foundation, the entire immense superstructure is more or less rapidly transformed.' (2) The nature of sport can therefore be expected to alter with any change to a new socio-economic formation.

These ideological considerations had major implications for Soviet thinking in regard to the broad concept of 'physical culture', embracing sport, physical education, health and hygiene education, civil defence and physical exercise.

First, sport with its broad relevance to education, health, culture and politics, and its capacity to mobilise people (predispose them towards change) could, it was felt, uniquely serve the purpose of nation-building and help foster national integration. Sport is uniquely suited to this role in that it extends to and unites wider sections of the population than probably any other social activity; it is easily understood and enjoyed, cutting across social, economic, educational, ethnic, religious and language barriers; it permits emotional release (reasonably) safely and is easily adapted to support educational, health and social welfare objectives.

Second, physical culture is regarded as equally important with mental culture in education and has to be treated as such both for the all-round, harmonious development of the child and, ultimately, for the health of the society. Inasmuch as mental is on a par with physical culture in human development, it follows that talent in physical activities should be treated no differently from talent in such mental activities as art, music and science. In other words, a budding gymnast, say, should be regarded no differently from a promising ballet dancer, and should be given every opportunity to develop her or his gifts, both for self-fulfilment and for the enjoyment of the community. This is a different philosophy to that dominant in many Western societies where the early cultivation of talent in sport, though not in music, has long been hampered by prejudice against early specialisation of children in sport. Thus, Britain, Canada and the USA only established their first sports boarding schools in the last decade.

Both the above-mentioned tsarist and ideological legacy naturally became entangled with the political, military and economic needs of the young Soviet state. In fact, the 'revolutionary imperative' of the first four years of the new state's existence led to mass nationalisation not only of industry, but of sport too, so that by the end of the War Communism period in 1921 not a single private, non-state sports club remained. Nor was the New Economic Policy period (1921-1928) to resurrect any. From 1917, therefore, Soviet sport has been entirely state-run for utilitarian purposes and employed as an <u>agent of social change</u>, with such functions as raising physical and social health standards, socialising people into the new system of values, encouraging people in rapid transition to identify themselves with wider communities (including the 'nation') and, after World War II, facilitating international recognition and prestige. This is a pattern and purpose of sport that predominates in many modernising societies and contrasts strongly with the development of sport in capitalist society.

99

Figure 4.1: Sports rankings and titles

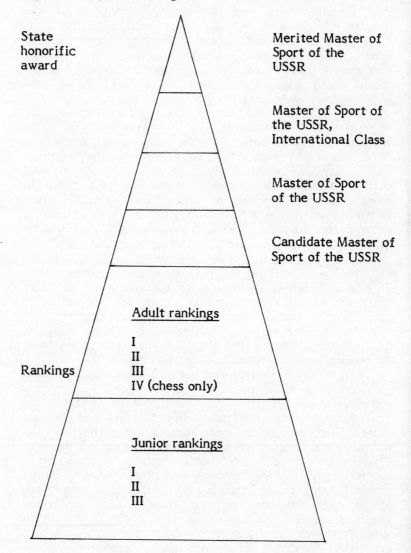

State honorific award — Merited Master of Sport of the USSR

Master of Sport of the USSR, International Class

Master of Sport of the USSR

Candidate Master of Sport of the USSR

Rankings

Adult rankings

I
II
III
IV (chess only)

Junior rankings

I
II
III

It was in the mid-1930s that the Soviet leadership took the decision to stratify in sport, to distinguish a more or less professional group of athletes from the mass. This was in keeping with the country's social development and its concomitant official values: in industry and agriculture, reward and prestige went to the peredoviki - workers and teams that attained the best results. Ordinary people were to be inspired by the efforts of heroes with whom they could identify. (3)

In 1935 the Soviet government created voluntary sports societies (dobrovolnye sportivnye obshchestva) based on the trade unions (Spartak for white-collar workers; Lokomotiv for railway workers; Torpedo for car workers, etc.) which, together with Dinamo (sponsored and financed by the security services) and clubs of the armed forces, formed full-time professional 'teams of masters' to compete in the nationwide cup and league tournaments instituted in 1936. One of the principal tasks of the sports societies was to act as a catalyst in raising standards through rational organisation and competition, to act as 'transmission belts' for potential talented athletes. Once these were discovered, it was then necessary to categorise and institutionalise them according to level of ability in a particular sport and to give them an incentive and special amenities to realise their potential. For this purpose a uniform rankings system (vsesoyuznaya yedinaya klassifikatsiya) was introduced in 1937, with rankings decided by times, distances or weights recorded in a particular event and/or success in competition. Figure 4.1 illustrates the rankings and titles pyramid as it exists today. Once the Master of Sport level is attained, the athlete may apply himself or herself full time to sport, unencumbered by a job of work outside the sporting vocation.

Prior to World War II, almost all sports competition was conducted within the USSR. With the conclusion of the War and the decision to join international sports federations and the IOC (in 1951), the appearance had to be given that Soviet athletes complied with the definition of an 'amateur'. It transpired that proficient athletes would be classified either as a student or as a commissioned serviceman under the sponsorship of a sports society or club. In the case of the country's two best endowed societies, Dinamo and the Central Army Sports Club, the athlete would hold a commission, but not be expected to undergo any form of military service.

101

Having proved itself militarily at enormous cost in the War, the Soviet Union now felt the need to prove itself in non-military spheres. Given the limited opportunities elsewhere, sport seemed to offer a suitable medium for pursuing this goal; it was an area in which the USSR did not have to take second place to the West. Of course, this policy presupposed a level of skill in a wide range of sports superior to that existing in the leading Western states. On the eve of war, Soviet sport was approaching that level in several sports; in some, it had actually reached it. This trend was reinforced after the war by mobilising the total resources of the entire sports system, by creating full-time, well-remunerated athletes and teams, with a back-up system of detecting and nurturing sports talent. It is due to this system that the USSR soon became the most successful and versatile nation in the history of sport, particularly at the Olympic Games.

TALENT SEEKING

The search for talent in sport is based on a centrally-planned (and, today, computer-assisted) system of selecting, testing, grading and sifting over a long period. The overall approach to talent-identification tends to focus on establishing a model for each sport and event. This is made up of statistical data from a large number of domestic and foreign world-class athletes in the particular sport. It includes information on performance at various ages, the rate of progress, the ideal physical profile, and so on. The planners are thus able to set approximate standards for what can be expected from a potentially gifted athlete at a certain biological age.

From a recent study I made of over a hundred Soviet studies of talent selection and forecasting, the data they use typically include the following: (4)

anthropological measurements (height, weight, arm reach)
general physical performance (speed, strength, power, endurance, mobility, agility)
performance levels in particular sports (swimming, sprinting, long jump, etc.)
sport-event-specific performance ability - for example, in track and field:

100 and 200m - speed endurance
400 to 1500m - aerobic and anaerobic endurance
3000 to 10,000m - aerobic endurance
hurdles - speed, speed endurance, mobility, agility
jumps - power, speed
throws - power, strength
rate of progress in these indicators.

Once a model has been created for a sport, the relevant standards and anticipated rate of progress are used to select potential talent in <u>three</u> major stages over four or five years. (5) The age at which the youngster is involved in the system depends on the sport, ranging from 7-8 in swimming, gymnastics, tennis and figure-skating to 12-13 in boxing and cycling, and 13-14 in shooting and weightlifting.

Stage 1: basic selection

This takes place either at school during the PE lesson or at the various non-residential sports schools. Since the PE lesson is fairly uniform throughout the country, it is relatively easy to measure potential talent at this point. The main standards observed at this stage normally include height and weight; speed (30m from standing start); endurance (12-15 min run); work capacity (step tests); power (standing long jump); and sport-specific tests for performance level and technique efficiency.

Stage 2: preliminary selection

This occurs some 18 months after Stage 1. Assessment is based on a number of factors: progress made in physical ability and the sport-specific tests, rate of physical growth, biological age, psychological aptitude, etc. At this stage it is usual to guide youngsters towards a particular sport or group of sports. There is some reluctance in the USSR, though less in the GDR and Rumania, to specialise early, on the grounds that the rates of motor development tend to be erratic.

Some youngsters are eliminated after the preliminary selection has been made, but they will be given another chance to prove their worth a year later when they are reassessed. Those found suitable in the second assessment will join the training squads at the sports schools until the final selection takes place.

Stage 3: final selection

This occurs about three or four years after Stage 1, usually at age 13-14, depending on the sport. For example, in most track and field events it is felt that, on average, 12-14 for boys and 11-13 for girls are the best ages to make performance predictions so as to guide youngsters towards a particular event. Based once more on the ideal model parameters of a particular sport, the final selection takes account of:

standards attained in a specific sport (eg times and distances in running, jumping, throwing)
rate of progress in the sport
stability of performance (how often good performances occur)
results of physical capacity tests
results of event/sport-specific performance capacity tests
results of psychology tests
anthropometric measurements (eg height for basketball, arm reach for discus, agility for gymnastics).

Once the person is identified as possessing potential talent, he or she will normally be offered a place at a residential sports school. It is, nonetheless, evident from the literature that a number of problems constantly exercise the minds of coaches and medical specialists who plan these schedules. One problem is the lack of satisfactory evidence to separate true from apparent potential. Young people may attain a high standard of test results at a certain age, yet fail to reach the forecast performance. This problem is underlined by the high drop-out/rejection rate at sports schools; over half of those selected in the early stages of talent identification for sports schools do not attain the anticipated performance levels. (6) A second problem is the varying rates of progress in physical performance indicators, with surges in some at certain ages and relatively slow development in others. Some research findings show that such unstable progress occurs in speed and power between 12 and 15, in muscle endurance between 14 and 15 and between 16 and 17, in strength between 13 and 16, and in endurance between 12 and 14. (7)

Thirdly, there is still much disagreement about the most suitable age at which to commence sport-specific training. Youngsters often display good all-round ability in the 10-12 age group, and there appear to be dangers in early specialisation before 13; some specialists, however, insist that guidance to take up a particular sport or event is necessary before 12 in order to ensure efficient skill development in the more complex technical events, like tennis, figure skating, gymnastics and some track and field events.

The final point to make is that many tests would certainly appear relatively primitive to Western coaches. Most tests in the early selection stages are simple field tests, and the PE teacher's or coach's eye often provides the most ready information. Of course, the multi-stage process of testing, with potential talent being subjected to more sophisticated testing at later stages, undoubtedly improves the reliability of physical performance tests. While the reliability of initial testing is reckoned to be about 30%, the reliability of the rate of progress during the first 18 months is said to be about 77%. (8)

SPORTS SCHOOLS

Once the young athlete is identified as possessing potential talent, he or she will be invited to join one of the various types of sports school. Here the budding athlete will enjoy certain privileges. Apart from expert guidance from trained coaches and regular examination and advice from sports medical specialists, he or she will enjoy completely free tuition and coaching, all costs being covered for training camps, and some educational privileges - eg being given a longer period to complete educational courses or receiving an individually-tailored course (as almost all student 'master' athletes do at the various institutes of physical culture).

Young people, then, who wish to pursue a sport seriously and to develop their talent may do so at one of the several types of school for gifted athletes (see Figure 4.2). At the base of the pyramid is the children's and young people's sports school (detsko yunosheskaya sportivnaya shkola) which young people can attend outside their normal

Figure 4.2: Types of sports school in the USSR

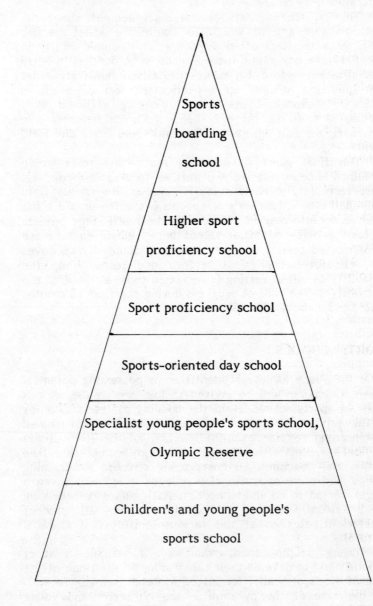

school hours (they are, in fact, 'clubs' in the Western sense). The first such school was said to be the Alexeyev School, opened in Leningrad in 1936.

Until 1981, these were entirely for children with some sort of promise or inclination for a particular sport. However, as part of the drive to involve more children in regular and active sports participation, a distinction was made in 1981 between such schools 'for all girls and boys irrespective of age and special talent for a particular sport' and those with the 'necessary amenities and qualified staff for training promising athletes.' (9) Henceforth, the former would be known as children's and young people's sports schools, while the latter would be called children's and young people's sports schools, Olympic reserve. The education authorities are responsible for financing and administering the former - roughly half the total number of such schools, while the sports societies, especially Dinamo and the Central Army Sports Club, are responsible for the latter.

Altogether there were some 7,500 such schools with an enrolment of over 3,500,000 children in the mid-1980s - a 2.5-fold increase since 1970 (see Table 4.1). As the table shows, an attempt is made to spread the net as widely as possible, both to catch all potential talent and to distribute facilities fairly evenly among the farflung areas of the Soviet Union. The fourth largest Republic, Belorussia, for example, is divided into six regions, each of which had 35 such schools with an average of 50 coaches per school in 1985, when the author visited several of them. Each school catered for an average of six sports: for example, the Republican School of Olympic Reserves in the capital, Minsk, had some 800 children in six sections: chess, gymnastics, handball, tennis, volleyball and waterpolo (the chess section having six separate groups under three instructors).

Children are normally considered for such schools on the recommendation of their school PE teacher or at the request of their parents. Sports newspapers also carry items advertising entry trials to the schools. Attendance and coaching are free. While most take children at the age of 11, for some sports they may accept them earlier or later, depending on the parameters laid down by the USSR Sports Committee. (10) In recent years, the age limits have gone down: in 1977, for example, the Moscow Dinamo CYPSS started up a gymnastics section for children between 4 and

Table 4.1: Children's and young people's sports schools and their enrolment, selected years 1970–1983

Republic	1970		1975		1983	
	No. of schools	Enrolment (thous.)	No. of schools	Enrolment (thous.)	No. of schools	Enrolment (thous.)
Russia	1919	6158	2731	8398	3625	18785
Ukraine	517	2185	789	2815	1084	4927
Belorussia	207	617	356	1021	454	1766
Uzbekistan	166	592	241	884	439	1678
Kazakhstan	318	1202	425	1623	560	2673
Georgia	107	363	132	466	200	762
Azerbaidzhan	73	262	78	262	193	826
Lithuania	72	273	105	384	134	649
Moldavia	84	279	84	277	121	546
Latvia	71	206	80	224	90	536
Kirgizia	53	232	74	293	101	535
Tadzhikistan	49	229	76	319	108	555
Armenia	65	294	95	396	159	712
Turkmenia	53	172	76	202	101	358
Estonia	59	170	54	180	57	287
USSR (total)	1813	13234	5396	17767	7426	35595

Source: Zhenshchiny i deti v SSSR (Moscow, 1985), pp. 150–1.

Table 4.2: Training programme of a gymnastics school

Name of Group	Number of Groups	Age Boys	Age Girls	Number of Pupils in Group	No. of Sessions Per Week Boys	No. of Sessions Per Week Girls	Length of Each Session Boys	Length of Each Session Girls
Preparatory	3	9	8	15	2	2	2	2
'Young Gymnast'	3	10	9	15	3	3	2	2
3rd Rank	3	12	11	12	3	4	3	2
2nd Rank	2	13	12	8	4	3	3	3
1st Rank	2	15	13	6	4	4	4	3.5
Candidate Master of Sport	1	17	14	4	5	5	4	3.5
Master of Sport	1	18	15	3-4	5	5	4	3.5

Source: Tipovoe polozhenie o detsko-yunosheskoi sportivnoi shkole (DYUSSH) (Moscow, 1970), p. 25.

109

6, the children attending three times a week - though training appeared (to the author) to be fairly general. (11)

Each leading soccer and ice hockey club (soccer is the major spectator sport in summer, ice hockey in winter) runs its own specialist 'nursery', providing a full course of training for promising young boys from the ages of 6 and 7 - these lower age parameters, too, falling from 9 and 10 in recent years.

The USSR Sports Committee lays down typical conditions of work for all the sports schools. The programme for special gymnastics schools gives some idea how serious the training and attendance are taken (see Table 4.2). Not all the schools in practice observe the Statute. For example, during several study visits to gymnastics schools over the last decade, the author noted that in Minsk and Leningrad, 7 year olds attended the gymnastics sections four times a week, arriving for each two-hour daily session at 9 am (they attended normal secondary schools on the second shift in the afternoons). The 11 year olds attended six days a week for three-hour sessions. The annual cycle of training consisted of preparatory work for the first three months of the year, followed by eight months of competitive gymnastics (ten internal and 22 external competitions) and one month of transitional work. The weekly timetable was as follows:

Monday - introductory work, comprising some 500 exercises
Tuesday - heavy training
Wednesday - heavy training
Thursday - light training
Friday - medium training
Saturday - heavy training, followed by a sauna
Sunday - day off.

Given that fairly rigorous schedule, it is perhaps hardly surprising that the drop-out rate in Minsk was relatively high: of the initial intake of 330, only 10% survived two years later. (12)

While initial testing of candidates was confined to height, weight, the parents' (and grandparents') physical measurements, and the children's gymnastics results, it later became more thorough as the gymnasts underwent extensive tests at the city sports clinic. The tests covered heart, blood, urine and muscle tissue. Besides access to the more specialised sports clinic in the city, the Minsk school also had its own medical treatment centre on the premises. While this is not always the case with all such sports schools, they do seem to be well served with both qualified (four- or five-year degree) coaches and sports doctors.

The principal aim of the sports schools is to use the best of the country's limited resources to give special and intensive coaching to children in a particular sport so that they may become proficient, gain a ranking and graduate to a national, Republican or city team. An examination of the sports pursued at the specialist sports schools leaves no doubt that the chief targets are the Olympic sports. The sports practised most in the schools are track and field, basketball, gymnastics, volleyball, swimming and skiing. (13)

The specialist schools are naturally provided with the best resources in the country: of the 65,000 full-time coaches in 1982, over half were working in the sports schools. Altogether, some 50,000 coaches and sports doctors were operating in the schools in the mid-1980s. (14) It is, moreover, the prescribed duty of the country's full-time athletes to undertake regular coaching and to give displays in the schools. Another advantage of the schools is that they have access to facilities, particularly for technical sports, that are generally in short supply. In 1982, for example, over 80% of the country's figure skaters and high divers, most of the swimmers and a third of all gymnasts pursued their sports in these schools. (15)

Another type of school is the sport-oriented day school (obshcheobrazovatelnaya shkola s sportivnym profilem), which combines a normal school curriculum with sports training - on the model of the foreign-language oriented schools. Then come the sports proficiency (shkola sportivnovo sovershenstvovaniya) and the higher sports proficiency (shkola vysshevo sportivnovo sovershenstvovaniya) schools, which provide extra-curricular training for schoolchildren and students on short-term (usually three months) vacation courses. The distinction between them is normally one of age - students between 16 and 18 attend the former, those 18 and over the latter.

At the apex of the pyramid are the sports boarding schools (sportivnaya shkola-internat). The USSR opened its first sports boarding school 'on an experimental basis' in the Central Asian city of Tashkent in 1962 - on the model of similar schools founded a few years earlier in the GDR. (16) In East Germany, four such schools (Kinder- und Jugendsportschule) had come into existence in 1952 (in

111

Berlin, Leipzig, Brandenburg and Halberstadt) following a government decree in 1951 - just two years after the GDR's foundation. By 1983, the GDR had 20 residential sports schools - though half the Soviet total in that year, they amounted to eight times more in per capita terms. (17)

It was only in 1970 that a special Soviet government resolution put the seal of approval on such schools in the USSR, by which time 20 existed, distributed about the Republics. (18) By 1984, there were 40 sports boarding schools with an enrolment of 15,121 pupils - a mean of 378 pupils per school. (19) Each school practises an average of seven-eight sports; all the sports are Olympic except chess (featured at one school, in Baku, home of the reigning world chess champion, Garry Kasparov), although the Olympic sports of shooting and sailing are not included. (20) The schools are run and financed jointly by the USSR Ministry of Education and the USSR Committee on Physical Culture and Sport (Sports Committee) attached to the USSR Council of Ministers. Local supervision is the joint responsibility of the Republican education ministries and sport committees.

They follow other specialised boarding schools (eg mathematical, musical, artistic) in adhering to the standard curriculum for ordinary secondary schools, but have an additional specialised study-load in sports theory and practice. Their aim is for pupils to obtain the school-leaving certificate in addition to proficiency in a particular sport. Boarders are accepted from between 7 and 11 depending on the sport, and stay on until the age of 18 - a year longer than at ordinary secondary schools (to enable them to cover the academic curriculum). Room and board, as well as coaching fees and travel expenses to competitions, are paid for by the state. Boarders also have the advantage of a special nutritious diet: at the Tashkent school, it was reported that the daily food expenditure of the school per pupil amounted to 1 ruble 64 kopeks, virtually double that (84 kopeks) at ordinary boarding schools. (21)

Boys and girls are normally invited to the schools on the basis of their performance in Republican school games, though some are attracted by advertisements placed in the sports press. Following the decision to expand such schools in 1981, a number of advertisements appeared in the daily newspaper Sovetsky sport. (22) Thus, one advertised for:

13-15 year old talented throwers: boys at least 185cm, girls 175cm. You are invited to come to Moscow for three-day trials. To take part you should let us know your name, date of birth, height, weight, sports results and your school record. Written permission from your parents is essential ... Those who are successful will be invited to continue their studies in secondary sports-profile boarding schools of Olympic training centres, free of charge. The training will be under the supervision of senior coaches of the USSR throwing team. (23)

It is a measure of the need to attract sufficient candidates that this advertisement was made in the form of a letter from the country's leading throwers (Melnik, Chizhova, Lusis, Bondarchuk, Sedykh, Kula and Kiselyov).

Once at the school, allocation of periods to sport in the timetable rises with each successive year of the course. For example, at a sports boarding school I visited in Tallin in 1981, 12 year olds in the gymnastics section spent 25 hours per six-day week on standard school subjects, two on swimming, two on general physical education and eight hours on gymnastics. In the top form, at 18, they devoted 23 hours a week to sport, including 19 hours of gymnastics. Roughly the same number of hours had to be spent on academic work. Despite these rigorous schedules, it is frequently asserted that pupils at sports boarding schools have a better-than-average health and academic record: the physical and mental aspects apparently supplement and reinforce each other. (24)

While some of the schools are well-equipped, some have relatively poor or no sports facilities at all. The Tallin school commanded three gymnasiums, a 25m indoor swimming pool, a ski centre, a track and field stadium with tartan track, and courts and fields for a variety of games. The Tashkent school grounds cover an area of 20 hectares and include a three-hall wing for gymnastics, indoor and outdoor swimming pools, and an indoor running track. (25) On the other hand, the Leningrad sports boarding school that I visited in 1980 had no sports facilities at all and had to rent them (though facilities were planned). Similarly, it was reported that the Frunze school, founded in 1968, had no sports amenities and its pupils had to train in a local sports club on even days and a physical culture institute on odd days, both at the other end of the city. (26) About the same time, children at the Pervomaisky District sports boarding school in Moscow had to travel to other parts of the city in order to use amenities like a swimming pool and indoor track and field stadium. (27) Doubtless, such a situation will improve as sports construction catches up with boarding school creation.

The motive for establishing the sports boarding schools has been the conviction that giftedness in sport has to be developed at an early age if it is to have an opportunity to blossom to the full. This is especially so in such sports as track and field, swimming, gymnastics and figure skating, where early specialisation would seem to be essential to the attainment of high standards and success in international competition. The three sports of track and field, gymnastics and swimming together account for nearly two-thirds of all medals at the summer Olympic Games.

It is no secret that the schools are expected to produce Olympic champions and that they have a political as well as an educational purpose:

> The sporting vocation has a practical importance not for mass sport, but for specialised sports schools in such disciplines as track and field, gymnastics, swimming, team games, figure skating, skiing and speed skating - ie in sports that constitute the basis of the Olympic programme. In assessing the significance of sport in international competition, we should remember that, while world and European championships are very important, victory at the Olympics acquires a political resonance. (28)

The point being made is that the Olympic Games carry more publicity and more national prestige. They are regarded by some as <u>the</u> measure of a nation's health and vitality. They are, further, the only visible sphere in which the USSR and other socialist states have overtaken the major capitalist powers.

It is thus regarded by many concerned with sports excellence as advantageous to bring children with an instinctive aptitude for sport into the 'controlled' environment of a residential school, where they are provided with the best coaches and amenities, nurtured on a special diet, supervised and tested regularly by medical staff, and stimulated by mutual interest and enthusiasm.

All the same, the schools are not without their open critics: some object that they lack depth and cannot produce a sustained flow of world-class athletes; the only answer, they say, is to provide more facilities for the population at large. After all, the number of children attending these and other types of sports schools amount only to just over 3% of all schoolchildren. (29) Other detractors have decried the marked acceptance of privilege implicit in the very existence of the schools. The respected economist Professor Birman, had a letter published prominently on the front page of Sovetsky sport, recalling Lenin's words that 'libraries should take pride in the number of readers they attract, not the rare books they have in their repositories.' Surely, Prof Birman writes, 'Lenin's words apply equally to sport?' (30)

The schools are also accused of encouraging the formation of an elite based on the luck of nature's draw and thereby perpetuating original inequalities rather than properly compensating for the lottery of birth. Some educationists are concerned about the study load imposed upon the children and the efficacy of combining mathematics and soccer, and the possibility of academic work being overshadowed. In a frank article in the weekly youth magazine Sobesednik, the former ice hockey star Yevgeny Zimin writes that he must 'confess with shame how frivolously I treated my studies ... apart from ice hockey I knew nothing and so could only count later on work in a sports organisation ... Although athletes are a strong breed, they aren't able to defend themselves and are prey to those coaches and sports administrators who cultivate them in hot-house conditions so that they are unsuited to real life.' (31)

The biggest stumbling block in the early stages of promoting sports boarding schools was parental opposition to giving up their children to the schools. One source admitted in 1971 that 'the sports boarding schools so far do not show the slightest popularity among parents - for various reasons. First, parents don't like the word internat (boarding school), perhaps because of its association with institutionalised care of the deprived. Then the word 'sport' puts them off. They find it embarrassing to tell the neighbours that 'my Sasha is in a sports school'. One parent is quoted as telling her neighbour that her daughter was in a special 'physics' rather than 'physical culture' school. (32)

Largely owing to such parental opposition, the Minsk sports boarding school was on the verge of closing down in 1971, and the situation was just as precarious in several others. The soccer boarding school (with some 100 pupils) in Voroshilovgrad, attached to the 1972 soccer champion club

Zarya, had trouble getting started, but not from parents. It met opposition from coaches at children's and young people's sports schools who were afraid of losing some of their charges. (33)

In recent years, particularly encouraged by the new atmosphere of openness (glasnost), the Soviet media have featured increasing criticism of elite sport and the privileges and 'distortions' resulting from the strong accent on sports excellence. A number of publications have drawn attention to the lack of sports facilities for the general public and the low level of participation in sport by young people. Others have focused attention on the unsavoury outcome of a 'win at all costs', 'obsession with medals' mentality, not to mention the corruption, bribery and fixed results, especially in soccer matches. (34)

In a revealing investigation of special schools generally, the editor of the Moscow youth newspaper Moskovsky komsomolets, writing in the Komsomol monthly Molodoi kommunist, reported on the excellent teaching, good relations between pupils and teachers and the active involvement in social work at such schools; however, for many pupils the schools are 'merely a means to the cherished goal of entering a prestigious university, of travel abroad and a profitable marriage.' (35) Another journal, Smena, featured an article by a teacher in Andizhan in Uzbekistan, where one of the first sports boarding schools began in the early 1960s: she wrote that 'it has become a status symbol to attend special schools ... and to go there in a Volga car.' (36)

The monthly sports journal, Sport v SSSR, has complained of the 'strict regimentation and the deprivation of many of childhood's joys, the numerous trips, lengthy training camps, hotel stays, separations from family and school, as well as the fact of belonging to a sports elite which gives rise in some youngsters to a sense of superiority over their peers. All this, many educationists believe, leads to moral impairment.' (37) Early specialisation and intensive training at the age of 5, 6 and 7 have come under attack, especially after the publication of a study of children's sports schools in Kazan, showing that 'there was practically no difference between beginners and the top athletes when it came to the number of intensive practices and sessions to develop particular skills.' (38)

In a blistering attack on a number of disgraced coaches, athletes and administrators, the weekly magazine Ogonyok in early 1987 wrote that 'No medals can replace what is the most valuable thing of all - a human being ... No matter how sweet the victory, it should never become an end in itself, a desperate need to do anything to attain it.' (39) It was the concentration on 'future champions' that was said to be the cause of as many as 56,400 youngsters giving up gymnastics in 1986: 'whole numbers of boys and girls keen to do some basic gymnastics ... get turned away so that a handful of gifted children can be trained in very complex routines.' (40)

The nature of such comments and the apparent effectiveness of parental opposition suggest a fairly low status for sport as a vocation, at least in the eyes of an important section of the public. While officials may see in the sports boarding schools a more efficient way of producing champions and controlling the free time of young people, using it for sports training, many parents would seem to dislike the idea of greater state control over their children than is absolutely necessary through attendance at ordinary schools and the Pioneers. The mood of glasnost also appears to be more in favour of sport for all than special privileges for the gifted.

Nonetheless, after a period of teething troubles the schools of sporting excellence, particularly the boarding schools, do seem to have gained a permanent niche in the sports and education system, probably because they have delivered the goods: confirmed the USSR as the world's best all-round sporting nation. And trends in other countries, often inspired by the Soviet and other socialist state (GDR, Cuba, China) treatment of sports giftedness, seem to be towards the spread of such schools. Purists may well argue that this is yet another step in the race for irrational glory that should find no place in a socialist society. The practitioners, on the other hand, may consider it a natural and rational development in a centrally-planned state to concentrate resources to maximum effect in order to win victories in today's highly competitive, specialised world of sport.

CONCLUDING REMARKS

By contrast with the USSR and most other economically developed socialist states, the provision for sporting excellence in the Western world differs considerably both between nations and between 'amateur' and 'professional'

117

sports.

Although there have been tentative efforts to start sports boarding schools (the USA and Canada have one each; Britain started up its first one, for soccer, in 1984; France and West Germany have six each), they cannot measure up in any serious way to the coordinated, ramified network of free sports schools in the East. Sports rankings exist in some Western states for a narrow range of sports (swimming, gymnastics, track and field), but screening, performance prediction, the application of science and medicine to sport all vary considerably in effectiveness over sports and nations, and often suffer from lack of coordination (if not outright hostility) between coaches, athletes, sports scientists, officials and government. Status, work conditions, certification and effectiveness of coaches also differ so widely that no generalisation is possible. For example, the USA hired its first full-time national coach in track and field in 1982, while Germany employed its first in 1913, and West Germany had 13, plus another 11, one in each of its federal states, in 1982. (41) While West German sports organisations began a coaching certification programme in 1974, it, like similar programmes elsewhere, is not compulsory; effectively, anyone can become a coach in the West.

In general in the Western world, the priority attachment of sport to 'cost-effectiveness' allied to the traditional amateur-elitist abhorrence of early sport specialisation have resulted in elite development often being left to the physical and moral resources of the individual athlete and coach, and in a stigma being attached to the cultivation of sporting talent on a par with, say, music and ballet. Neither inhibiting factor exists in the USSR. In fact, the Soviet leadership has used sport to help build a new society. Given such a key role, it could not be allowed to develop haphazardly in the hands of individual enthusiasts who made the playing of sport exclusive to a particular group, or commercial promoters whose interest was not sport or the community, but the profit they could make out of both. The Soviet utilitarian use of sport for political, economic, defence, integration and international purposes has resulted in a model that is being followed by a number of other developing countries throughout the world. It has also demonstrated that the highest realisation of human potential can most effectively be achieved through the planned application of society's resources.

NOTES

1.   Karl Marx, A Contribution to the Critique of Political Economy (Chicago, 1904), pp. 11-12.
2.   Ibid., p. 13.
3.   For a history of Soviet sport, see J. Riordan, Sport in Soviet Society (CUP, Cambridge, 1977).
4.   See J. Riordan, 'Sports medicine in the Soviet Union and the German Democratic Republic,' International Review of Social Science and Medicine, vol. 25, no. 1, (1987), p. 27.
5.   Four stages are generally used for the selection of youngsters for sports schools and top-level teams outside the schools. Here I omit Stage 4. See V. Filin, 'Organizatsiya i metodologiya sportivnovo otbora,' in V. Volkov, V. Filin, Sportivny otbor (Moscow, 1983), pp. 142-72.
6.   V. Volkov, V. Filin, 'Prognozirovanie sportivnykh dostizheniy,' in V. Volkov, V. Filin, Sportivny otbor (Moscow, 1983), p. 111.
7.   Ibid., p. 127.
8.   A.G. Dembo, Aktualnye problemy sovremennoi sportivnoi meditsiny (Moscow, 1980), p. 11.
9.   Sovetsky sport, 24 September 1981, p. 1.
10.   Volkov, Filin, 'Prognozirovanie ...' in Volkov, Filin, Sportivny otbor, p. 125.
11.   On the other hand, much criticism appeared in the press about 4 and 5 year olds being 'deformed' at a gymnastics school run by the coach I.I. Mametiev in the small Siberian town of Leninsk-Kuznetsky (which nonetheless produced a number of Soviet female champions - Maria Filatova and Larisa Komarova included). See Komsomolskaya pravda, 14 January 1976, p. 4.
12.   Personal communication during visits to the School in 1978, 1981, and 1985.
13.   V.P. Platonov, Podgotovka kvalifitsirovannykh sportsmenov (Moscow, 1986), p. 227.
14.   Figures given by the then Sports Committee Chairman, Sergei Pavlov, in Sovetsky sport, 14 November 1981, p. 1; and by Lev Markov, 'The doors are open to all,' Sport in the USSR, no. 5, (1985), p. 39.
15.   V. Balashov, 'Sportivnye shkoly,' Teoriya i praktika fizicheskoi kultury, no. 9, (1983), p. 50.
16.   Fizkultura i sport, no. 7, (1968), p. 5.
17.   Dieter Ehrich, 'Leistungssport in der DDR unter besonderer Berücksichtigung der Talentsuche und

Talentförderung,' in Die DDR. Breiten- und Spitzensport (Kopernikus Verlag, Munich, 1981), p. 32.

18.   Moskovskaya pravda, 26 February 1971, p. 4.

19.   Byulleten normativnykh aktov Ministerstva prosveshcheniya SSSR, 5 August 1983, Nos 94/95, pp. 36-44.

20.   Ibid., p. 43.

21.   Fizkultura i sport, no. 7 (1968), p. 6.

22.   See 'Vnimaniyn yunykh lyubitelei lyogkoi atletiki,' Sovetsky sport, 24 January 1982, p. 4; 'Prikhodite k nam uchitsya,' Sovetsky sport, 30 March 1982, p. 4; 'Yunye futbolisty!' Sovetsky sport, 24 March 1982, p. 4; 'Prikhodite k nam uchitsya,' Sovetsky sport, 31 March 1982, p. 4.

23.   'Priglashenie k konkursu metatelei,' Sovetsky sport, 18 February 1982, p. 4.

24.   Fizkultura i sport, no. 7 (1968), p. 6. A gymnastics school in Dnepropetrovsk claimed to show better academic results, as well as improved health and discipline, than 'ordinary' local schools - see Sovetsky sport, 13 September 1974, p. 2.

25.   Fizkultura i sport, no. 7 (1968), p. 5.

26.   This state of affairs was blamed on higher authorities: 'The boarding school would have long had everything necessary if people in high places, from the Ministry of Education to the Kirgiz Sports Committee, had displayed any real concern for their offspring' - see Sovetsky sport, 29 June 1974, p. 2.

27.   Sovetsky sport, 17 September 1971, p. 1.

28.   Teoriya i praktika fizicheskoi kultury, no. 5 (1968), p. 42.

29.   See Zhenshchiny i deti v SSSR (Moscow, 1985), pp. 106-114, and 150-1.

30.   Sovetsky sport, 18 October 1974, p. 1.

31.   Yuri Bychkov, 'Schastlivchik?' Sobesednik, no. 35 August 1986, p. 12.

32.   Moskovskaya pravda, 26 February 1971, p. 4.

33.   Sovetsky sport, 21 October 1972, p. 3.

34.   For soccer 'scandals', see Lev Filatov, 'O lzhefutbole,' Ogonyok, no. 44 (October 1986), pp. 26-7; Filatov, 'Dobroe imya futbola,' Ogonyok, no. 4 (January 1987), pp. 26-7; Oleg Petrichenko, 'Ne sotvori sebe kumira,' Ogonyok, no. 12 (March 1987), pp. 14-15.

35.   Pavel Gusev, 'Chtoby chitatel nam veril,' Molodoi kommunist, no. 5 (1987), pp. 36-7.

36.   Dina Gurvich, 'Nabolelo!' Smena, no. 20 (October 1986), p. 6.

37.   L. Kedrov, 'Sport v vozraste 6 let: za i protiv,' Sport v SSSR, no. 6 (1987), p. 27.

38.   Ibid.

39.   Stanislav Tokarev, 'Ne proigrat by cheloveka,' Ogonyok, no. 9 (February 1987), p. 20. The accompanying cartoon shows two strong men carrying a winner's podium over the heads of a mass of casual athletes.

40.   Boris Rogatin, 'Time to revitalise Soviet gymnastics,' Soviet Weekly, 1 August 1987, p. 14.

41.   A. Krüger and J. Casselman, 'A comparative analysis of top-level track and field coaches in the USA and West Germany,' Comparative Physical Education and Sport, no. 3 (1982), p. 22.

Chapter Five

EDUCATING THE DEAF-BLIND

Mike Lambert

DEAF-BLINDNESS

The loss of sight is a handicap which is to some extent within the comprehension of sighted people. The loss of hearing can possibly be conceived by those with full auditory function. But the loss or disruption of both sight and hearing, 'deaf-blindness', is surely a predicament beyond the imagination of all those who have full use of these two major distance senses.

The causes of deaf-blindness are many, varied and far from being fully understood. A major source of the condition, in some communities at least, is infection of the pregnant mother by the German measles or rubella virus, passed on to the foetus and damaging its pre-natal growth. Genetic syndromes may also be a cause, as in Usher syndrome, when deafness from birth is complicated by progressive visual deterioration in the teenage years. Viral infections such as measles, meningitis and polio can have serious effects on both senses; accidents add to the numbers, as do the very many children (up to 50 per cent in some studies) whose deaf-blind condition simply has no known origin. But even with such aetiological diversity the total number of deaf-blind individuals is comparatively small - research in the Scandinavian countries has suggested it is about 0.018 per cent of the population, the majority of these being adults suffering the normal ageing processes. Myers estimated 20,000 deaf-blind children throughout the 'developed' countries; (1) 1986 estimates gave the number in Britain at around 1,000.

The task of educators is intricate and difficult, a

process of giving human knowledge and skills to children who lack the capacity to acquire these spontaneously from their social and physical environment, children who have to be consciously taught if they are to learn. The complexity of this task, and the fact that only a small number of children are involved in each country, has meant that the field has developed and maintained an actively international character, with much inter-professional co-operation and sharing of ideas. This makes it all the more surprising that Western histories of deaf-blind education make little reference (and more usually no reference at all) to the education of deaf-blind children in the Soviet Union. Even a brief encounter with the material available - in Russian and in English - leads one quickly to the conclusion that the education of deaf-blind pupils in the Soviet Union is both long-established and, from a methodological point of view, highly developed. More detailed investigation can provide a fairly comprehensive picture of the history of Soviet deaf-blind education and its research concerns, together with some impression at least of its methodological practices. The perception gained, as this chapter will convey, is of a small but highly active and very significant field of Soviet defectology, one which not only displays all that is characteristic of Soviet practice with handicapped children, but one which is also pushing back the frontiers of defectological theory and practice with regard to some of its most complex and challenging children.

HISTORY

The first attempts to educate the deaf-blind in Russia were made in the early years of this century by a charitable body in St Petersburg. Postrevolutionary development of specialised methods and state provision for the deaf-blind was initiated by Ivan Sokolyansky (1889-1960). He had trained until 1913 in the education department of the Natural History Faculty at the St Petersburg Psycho-Neurological Institute. His early work was as a teacher and researcher in education of the deaf; after 1917 he became a leading figure in the development of special education in the Ukraine.

In 1923 Sokolyansky established a school-clinic for deaf-blind children in Kharkov, one of only 65 establishments for handicapped children in the whole of the country at that time. Maizel described it thus:

> Pupils were taught various subjects and handicrafts, general educational subjects and played different games, many of which demand great attention even on the part of normal children ... The children, of various ages, developed physically and mentally and lived and worked in a friendly community; the older inmates helped the staff in bringing up the little ones. (2)

By the 1930s work at the school-clinic was attracting international attention, one set of visitors being delegates to the 15th International Psychology Congress which took place in Moscow in 1935. But the war brought tragedy - the Nazis ransacked the building and murdered all but one or two of its pupils. Sokolyansky himself survived the war and restarted his work with the deaf-blind at the Defectology Institute in the 1950s. His contribution to defectology in general and to deaf-blind education in particular was considerable. He earned posthumous acclaim as 'the first defectologist to begin the construction of Soviet defectology on the basis of the scientific teachings of Ivan Sechenov and Ivan Pavlov on higher nervous activity'; his work with the deaf-blind was described as 'one of the most remarkable achievements of Soviet Science'. (3)

These words came from Sokolyansky's successor, Alexander Meshcheryakov (1923-74), who graduated from the psychology department of the Philosophy Faculty at Moscow University and worked from 1952 at the Defectology Institute. He took over as head of research into education of the deaf-blind in 1961, then during the thirteen years until his early death he made major methodological developments to Sokolyanksy's work, travelled widely (including visits to Britain in 1962 and 1967, and to Sao Paolo in 1975) and wrote over 80 research papers.

His closest colleague was a surviving pupil of the Kharkov school-clinic, Olga Skorokhodova (1914-82). Like all of the 'famous' deaf-blind, Olga Skorokhodova had become deaf and blind in childhood, after a period of unimpaired learning. Non-specialised teaching at a school in Odessa failed to halt her mental and behavioural decline. As she describes it, 'the older pupils, upbringers and teachers tried in all sorts of ways to amuse me - took me for walks, gave me various trinkets, beads, ribbons, spoiled me and tried to teach me.' (4)

Her admittance to Sokolyanksy's specialised school-clinic in 1925 changed her prospects. She completed primary and secondary schooling and after the war was reunited with Sokolyansky in Moscow. She moved on to higher education and eventually became a writer, researcher and figure of some popular renown. The process of her learning and her contributions to Soviet research on deaf-blindness have been a constant theme of Soviet literature in this field. Her book, How I Perceive, Imagine and Understand the World, attracted particular interest. It is a three-part work, a collection of notes made initially at the request of her educators, which recorded the process of her learning and the nature of her perceptions of objects, people, places and the arts. It caused her to become the most famous deaf-blind individual to reach normal levels of personal and academic attainment through specialised education in the Soviet period, the Soviet 'Helen Keller', typifying for many the developmental possibilities for severely handicapped individuals in the USSR.

Such possibilities started to be realised for greater numbers of deaf-blind children with the opening in 1963 of the Children's Home for Deaf-Blind Children in the monastery town of Zagorsk. The Home, run by the Ministry for Social Welfare but with full defectological input from the Ministry of Education, was - and still is - the centre for practice and curricular development in Soviet education of the deaf-blind. The building, standing back from the busy main road from Moscow into the town, is old, cramped and visually unremarkable. But its role is impressive - it has residential provision for 55 children 'with severe defects of sight and hearing, but with the potential for normal intellectual development.' (5) As a large specialised school for such children there is nothing quite like it anywhere in the world.

The 1970s saw the Home carry out its most celebrated work. An 'experiment' was initiated to extend the Zagorsk school curriculum for some of its more able pupils and to support four of these young people through degree courses at Moscow University. The purpose was to prove that deaf-blind individuals have the same potential for development as people with normal sight and hearing. The four students - Natasha Korneeva, Alexander Suvorov, Yuri Lerner and Sergei Sirotkin - graduated in 1977, an event described by Gurgenidze and Ilenkov as 'the climax to the scientific work of Sokolyansky and Meshcheryakov.' (6)

Other countries too can boast of deaf-blind individuals who have completed education at a high level - perhaps the Soviet Union is not altogether special in this respect. But like Olga Skorokhodova before them, the four graduates have continued to contribute to research on formation of the mind and imagination in deaf-blind people, an association which illustrates the close interaction of investigation and practice which has been a particular feature of Soviet work. This has found frequent expression in a range of publications. Sokolyansky's early writings can be found in reports of the Defectology Institute. A major collection of case studies Instruction and Upbringing of the Deaf-Blind described work at the Kharkov school-clinic and in post-war Moscow. (7) Meshcheryakov provided the most comprehensive picture of research-orientated practice in a major monograph, Deaf-Blind Children. (8) The most regular outlet for research papers has been the annual journal Defektologiya, formerly Spetsialnaya Shkola. Reports are also to be found in collections published by the Defectology Institute, and a wide range of topics has been covered elsewhere, from detailed scientific analysis in Soviet Neuropsychiatry to popular discourse in Children's Friend.

Meshcheryakov's monograph was subsequently published in English as Awakening to Life and is still available to the Western reader. (9) It describes and analyses specialised work over a score of years and conveys the striking humanitarian basis to Soviet work. It is also where Soviet belief in the hidden potential of so many deaf-blind children, expressed uncompromisingly by Sokolyansky in his early work, has found its clearest and most persuasive expression. Additional access to Soviet work for the English-language reader is provided by several published reports arising from visits by Soviet professionals to the West, among these Meshcheryakov's early but sophisticated report to the First International Seminar on Deaf-Blindness at Condover Hall School near Shrewsbury, England, (10) and a Moscow graduate's paper to the Helen Keller Centennial World Conference in New York. (11)

CURRENT CONCERNS

While the high profile which deaf-blind research enjoyed in the 1960s and 1970s has in recent years been somewhat reduced, very significant developments have continued to take place. Raisa Mareeva, the leading and long-standing research worker and defectologist in this field (she has worked on deaf-blind research at the Institute since the 1950s), published a comprehensive 80-page manual for parents, Upbringing and Instruction of Deaf-Blind Children in the Family (Mareeva, 1979). In a recent collection of studies from the deaf-blind laboratory at the Defectology Institute, Valery Chulkov, now head of the laboratory, has re-examined the work of Sokolyansky and Meshcheryakov in the light of present knowledge about the causes of deaf-blindness. (12) Research projects have been undertaken not just by the small team of workers at the Institute but also by experts in genetics and in mental retardation working elsewhere at the Institute, involving pupils in an experimental group of deaf-blind children at a Moscow school for the deaf, pupils at Zagorsk and schools elsewhere.

Curricular concerns are exemplified by the titles of recent reports in Defektologiya: 'Initial signs in deaf-blind children'; 'Drawing activity of a deaf-and-blind child acquiring verbal speech'; 'Development of Braille sign image with special means in blind-deaf children having residual vision'. But the major research task for Soviet professionals has been to meet the challenge faced similarly by professionals in the West, that is the implications for educational methodology and provision of changes in the aetiological patterns of deaf-blindness. With meningitis and other viral infectious diseases considerably reduced, the numbers of late-deafened-and-blinded children which resulted from them are lower too. With increasing awareness of other congenital and genetic syndromes and pre-natal damage, increased too are the children subject to a number of complex disabilities which include, amongst others, those of visual and hearing deficit. As a result, among those deaf-blind children with unimpaired (but drastically unfulfilled) mental capacity, significant numbers of children are identified whose sensory defects are compounded by additional organic mental defect. This latter group, while still able to benefit enormously from skilled and sensitive teaching, does not have that potential for full intellectual attainment which Sokolyansky and Meshcheryakov asserted with such confidence in their earlier work.

The process of differentiating between developmental delay and organic impairment is not new to Soviet defectology. Unlike British and American practice, Soviet work has always sought to diagnose mental deficiency on this basis, with investigation undertaken not to determine levels of previous attainment, but to assess the ability of children to learn from specialised teaching and to find evidence of proven damage to the central nervous system. Furthermore, provision itself has developed on the basis of this differentiation, with separate schooling for children with biological mental impairment (oligophrenia) and those whose intellectual delay is due to other factors, such as inappropriate upbringing and education (what Soviet specialists call 'pedagogical neglect') and the secondary effects of other primary defects.

There is no doubt that making this kind of differentiation in deaf-blind children stretches the expertise of Soviet defectologists to its limits. The effects of deaf-blindness are so severe that it is very difficult indeed to come to conclusions about the organic mental condition of individual children and to decide whether drastic deficiencies in learning stem from oligophrenia or from the secondary effects of the deaf-blind condition itself. This problem has been the major concern of research in the last decade. First of all, there has been the considerable task of refining identification of aetiological patterns of deaf-blindness. The Soviet Union has shared the Western experience of finding that a large percentage of deaf-blind children has no known cause of their condition. Studies by Bertyn from the genetics laboratory have investigated the aetiology of large groups of such children and adults and identified a wide range of complex genetically and non-genetically determined syndromes (a lower incidence of rubella in the Soviet Union appears to be the only significant difference from Western aetiological patterns.) Secondly, there is the need to identify organic mental defect in deaf-blind children, a process which has involved Bertyn, Pevzner (whose main interest over many years has been oligophrenia), and researchers from the deaf-blind laboratory itself.

These research studies have not been made out of academic or purely scientific interest. Refinement of differential diagnosis, say Soviet experts, improves the process of differentiated provision, the composition of an educational curriculum suited to the individual needs of children. This is a cornerstone of Soviet provision for handicapped children - education for deaf-blind children is no exception in this respect, despite the difficulties involved. Developments in provision in the last ten years have reflected these concerns. The Defectology Institute gives advice to parents of very young children, to specialised kindergartens for deaf children which provide early training to the deaf-blind, and to schools for the deaf which have individual or small groups of deaf-blind children among their pupils. Since the 1970s there has been a group of oligophrenic deaf-blind children at a children's home for blind oligophrenic children, the Golovenky Home, in Tula, south of Moscow. Such developments have enabled the Zagorsk Home to standardise its own procedures and clarify its educational objectives. The pre-school department there, described in such detail in Awakening to Life, no longer exists - pupils enter at the age of seven and complete eight years' education, with two further years of vocational training and continuing education. The Home's curriculum now aims to take its deaf-blind children through primary and, in many cases, through aspects of secondary education as well. Vocational training leads towards full-time employment, usually in large, self-financing industrial enterprises run by the All-Russia Association for the Blind in Zagorsk or in Sarapul (700 miles to the east) and accompanied by further educational opportunities in evening school classes.

But progress in providing services has been slow. The team of defectologists available to give advice appears to be desperately small. Identification of deaf-blind children in some areas of the country must still be a matter more of good luck than good management; the problems of false diagnosis of the deaf-blind as mentally handicapped are still daunting. Without comprehensive figures it is impossible to say with confidence how many deaf-blind children receive appropriate specialised education in the Soviet Union, but the impression is that it can only be a small proportion of the number of those who might benefit from it. The Zagorsk Home still awaits its new, larger premises to replace the overcrowded and basic facilities of its present building.

ASPECTS OF CURRICULUM AND METHODOLOGY

Despite these problems (problems shared, to a greater or lesser extent, by every Western country too), Soviet practice shows a depth of experience which most work elsewhere finds difficult to match. This experience has resulted in a complex methodology, based on confidence in the power of specialised education to bring about transformation of the deaf-blind child's psychological and behavioural state, to turn children still at the beginnings of learning away from an abnormal course of development and lead them towards levels of socialisation and intellectual attainment more normally associated with non-handicapped individuals. This chapter can do no more than state some of the general features of Soviet approaches.

Investigations by A.V. Yarmolenko in the 1940s and 1950s provided documentary evidence of the psychological predicament of deaf-blind children without specialised education. As Meshcheryakov describes:

> To an outside observer, they seem to be excluded from life ... Immobile and without any initiative, they can remain for hours in the same place or in an unchanged attitude. They do not use their sense of touch in order to reorientate themselves in space and to perceive new objects. They have failed to develop any habits, owing to which even the processes of eating, dressing and undressing, and satisfying the elementary needs can be begun only after a stimulus from the outside is given ... These children have no intercourse, which means they do not strive to get in touch with other human beings, do not seek them. (13)

The writings of Meshcheryakov, Mareeva and others have presented many similar examples of such behaviour in children before remediating measures were undertaken, including severe difficulties in feeding, sleeping, toileting and dressing, obsessive behaviour, stereotyped movements, extreme passivity, violence towards objects, people and self. Such problems are not easily overcome: 'A great deal of work and meticulous teaching are necessary to overcome the child's persistent passive-defensive reaction, to nurture natural needs, to get rid of inert patterns of movement and establish habits of normal behaviour.' (14)

Meshcheryakov identified the primary task of initial teaching to be the development of orientative reactions to the surrounding world. This meant teaching children to form 'images' of their surroundings, in particular of the objects in it, and to teach them the skills to do this independently. Thus: 'The world seems vacant and objectless ... before training begins'; (15) 'It is important right from the start to fill the void around such children with objects that create a stable familiar world for them', a world 'filled with things that have meaning, which they are able to use correctly, and which are correctly reflected in their consciousness.' (16) To do this it is not enough simply to encourage the use of touch to compensate for the sight and hearing which are lacking:

> It may all seem very simple; put certain objects into the child's hands; the child will then feel these objects and will thus form any number of desirable images of the surrounding world. However, experience has shown this to be impracticable ... If such a child is given some objects for 'investigation', it immediately drops them, without even attempting to 'find out' what they are. This is understandable since the objects given to the child have no meaning for it. (17)

Meshcheryakov saw the 'image' of objects to be not so much in their shape or material, as in their use. Children become familiar with objects connected with their practical activity when meeting their own self-felt needs:

> In the course of satisfying elementary physical necessities as, for instance, in the process of eating, a human being uses a number of tools, such as a spoon, fork, plate, etc ... In the process of this 'business' activity of the child's organism, the child is compelled to become acquainted with certain objects, for the simple reason that knowledge of the eating tools is a condition of receiving direct reinforcement (in this case, in the form of food) ... in the process of eating, these objects acquire a definite use for the organism, they become significant, and the child feels them by hand (emphases in the original). (18)

Socialisation starts to take place when the elementary skills of self-care are taught, not as 'a selection of unconnected skills', but as 'an integrated, uninterrupted stream of human behaviour.' (19) To do this the child's surroundings must be structured and stable. Events 'should follow each other in a strictly established order.' (20) The object environment must be sparse and unchanging. Crucial too is the role of the adults who deal with the child: 'The mind of a deaf-blind child only starts to develop when it enters into a relationship with an adult.' (21) In the words of the head of the Zagorsk Home: 'Only in the adult's hands can material experience become active and in this active state, and only in this active state, is it ready for assimilation by the child.' (22)

The case study of Lena G. in <u>Awakening to Life</u> provides graphic illustration of all these factors in the early training of a deaf-blind child:

> The first step towards teaching Lena to find her way about was to familiarise her with the corner in which she slept. Since the little girl was put to bed in a cot and covered up with a blanket, the drop-side of the cot filled in with netting was raised and lowered at regular intervals, she was soon to become acquainted with the bed and bed-clothes; she knew the pillow was soft and the metal head of the bed was hard. In practical terms she was familiar with her corner of the room almost from the outset of her stay at the Home. Special activities were organised for the child to extend her knowledge while making practical use of the objects around her. The teacher would take the little girl's hands in her own and then proceed to make the bed, to raise and lower the drop-side, lead the child along one side of the cot, letting her gain an idea of its size through feeling it; Lena would also climb under the cot and with her teacher's help familiarise herself with the bed-legs, the wheels at the bottom of the legs and then even move the bed. In this way she also investigated the space around the bed: the bedside locker, the rug by the bed where her slippers were laid out and the strictly defined place for the pot under the bed, etc. Lena was thus encouraged to familiarise herself with a new world in a systematic way. (23)

Self-care activities are only the start of what Soviet specialists have called the 'humanisation' of the deaf-blind child. Other activities, in particular play, drawing and modelling, broaden and refine the child's images, with attention paid not just to learning about objects but to nurturing feelings and attitudes as well. Mareeva has made this process clear in relation to play activities.

> In play the deaf-blind child actively studies and gets to know the surrounding world, thinks and creates within the limits of its age, reveals inclinations and interests

... play actively enables it to develop those qualities and habits which will in future have enormous significance for adaptation to life and work. (24)

Her suggestions for play activity are well-structured miniatures of human life using dolls and teddy bears. Among the developmental aspects noticeably and consciously advanced in them are the child's images of the surrounding world of objects and ordinary activity, gesture, imitation, speech and independent play activity. Very prominent too are moral concepts of kindness to others:

'Teddy Hurts His Paw'
... Taking a child's hand on which there was a scratch, the teacher drew attention to it. The child asked if it could be rubbed with cream (the teacher put ointment on it). Then the teacher explained that Teddy's paw was also hurting. Taking some cotton wool, a bowl and a little stick, the child spread 'ointment' on the paw and blew gently on it. When it came to putting a bandage on, the teacher explained how to use it. Some movements were done by teacher and pupil together, but the child finished tying it on her own ... (25)

Language controls, extends and organises the 'integrated vision' of human activity and lays the basis of human thought: 'The child's direct non-verbal knowledge, i.e. images of objects, actions, functions and qualities, are pre-systematised in accordance with the logic of language.' (26)
It is this aspect of teaching which has most clearly separated Soviet thinking from practices in Western countries, where 'communication' often appears as the be-all and end-all of teaching in the initial stages. Meshcheryakov warned that the deaf-blind child with a developed memory could learn a great deal of language without linking it to the real world around it. He called it 'training (circus-style) ... pupils to utter certain isolated phrases', 'word-skill' as opposed to 'true knowledge'. (27) At the Condover Conference he said that, 'In our view, language in the early stages only gives form to elements of human thought that have already taken shape in the context of practical behaviour involving objects ... Before forming a word orally, the child must know what the word means.' (28)
The forms of language taught are gesture, finger spelling ('dactylology'), speech, braille and print. Initial

gestures combine object and action and represent the movements of self-care activity. In dactylology (the one-handed finger spelling of the deaf) each word is fully spelt out and understood by those unable to see by placing one hand lightly on top of the 'speaking' hand and feeling its movements. Dactylology makes possible the prompt learning of written language forms - enlarged print for those with residual vision, braille for the totally blind. But Soviet literature has always claimed that the aim of language teaching is to teach oral speech. Western educators, more used to abandoning speech training in favour of manual systems of communication, in particular for the congenitally deaf-blind, find this hard to accept. However, examination of the timetable for third grade pupils (aged 10) at the Zagorsk Home shows that the Soviet claim is not just an expression of good intentions. As much as 45 per cent of lessons are devoted to the development of oral speech, ten lessons being specific work on the development of pronunciation, five more generally on the development of speech. Speech profiles in each classroom display the sounds mastered by each pupil.

Two other aspects of practice stand out. Firstly, there is an insistence that to be effective teaching must stem from the practical experiences of childhood. So play, modelling and drawing must examine and expand on these experiences as the source of children's learning about themselves as individuals, about their relationships with others and about their association with society at large. Secondly, the idea is frequently stressed that children in the early stages of learning are helped most effectively by pupils who are further along the path to full development, who guide them by example towards the socialised behaviour and practical skills of a civilised collective existence. Thus group spirit at Zagorsk is strong, strong enough to act as a motivational force in advancing the emotional, social and moral development of the Home's pupils.

The Zagorsk school timetable gives more clues to the Home's curricular concerns and expectations - reading, writing (in print or braille) and mathematics all form part of the ten-year-old pupil's six-day working week. In line with the rest of Soviet education, Meshcheryakov put forward manual labour as an essential part of the deaf-blind child's moral education: 'Teaching a child work skills and involving it in useful work is the only way to develop a full, rounded personality ... it is in work that a person's vital, essentially human characteristics take shape.' (29) As might be expected, group work, cooperation on a common task, work for the good of the Home and its pupils, all have particular significance. Meshcheryákov described how Tolya Ch. and Alik K. made two toys for the school's nursery group, three other pupils made shelves for the store room, and Alexei B. and Seriozha B. repaired furniture for the younger children. A visitor to the Zagorsk Home today is likely to be served jam made by the children from fruit grown in the garden.

PHILOSOPHICAL IMPLICATIONS

Many years' experience in specialised settings has given Soviet teachers a high measure of confidence in the effectiveness of their methods. The achievements of the Zagorsk school in helping pupils - apparently with some regularity - to reach the developmental levels of the non-handicapped suggest that such confidence is justified. But the significance of deaf-blind education has not been confined in Soviet thinking to the successful nature of much of the work. Added significance has been attributed to this field for the light it is said to cast on the process of learning and formation of personality in the non-handicapped individual as well.

The basis for this claim lies in the premise, adopted wholeheartedly (and at times to extremes) by Soviet deaf-blind teaching, that a person learns exclusively from his social environment and not at all from biological inheritance. Meshcheryakov wrote that 'Human behaviour is shaped entirely in ontogenesis. It is the result of the interaction between the individual and society, the result of upbringing on the part of other people.' (30) With the deaf-blind the lack or severe disruption of sight and hearing precludes any learning without special adult intervention - for such children the environment is 'cut off', learning cannot take place, their world is a 'barren desert' (31) or, as Meshcheryakov put it, they are 'without a human psyche.' (32) The task for the educator is therefore considerable. It is to teach everything, including the many aspects of behaviour and thought which a normal child picks up incidentally, unnoticed by his teachers and those around him, in short to 'mould' a human personality. Adults become the channel for all information and learning, the source of all development; moreover, the 'process of the mind's emergence and development is slowed down' and can be studied. (33) The eminent writer Maxim Gorky summed it up thus: 'Deaf-blindness is the most extreme test put before us ... one which enables us to probe one of the most complex and awe-inspiring phenomena - the inner mechanism of emergent human consciousness in the objective relationships which mould consciousness.' (34)

Dr Meshcheryakov, who was fond of revising standard Western observations on the education of the deaf-blind, had a particularly memorable metaphor which encapsulated the materialist basis of Soviet deaf-blind teaching. It was in response to a Western observation, commonly expressed with reference to Helen Keller, which compared teaching of the deaf-blind with finding the key to a safe - once the safe is opened, the riches enclosed are revealed. Meshcheryakov agreed only up to a point. Yes, find the key, he said, open the safe. But when the safe is opened, it is found to be empty. The task of the educator, he claimed, is to fill the safe, to fill it with 'the patterns of human thought and behaviour in all their rich diversity.' (35)

CONCLUSION

It is unfortunate that Dr Meshcheryakov's work, indeed the expertise of Soviet deaf-blind teaching as a whole, has attracted so little attention in the West. One reason may simply be the limited nature of the 'deaf-blind' field. Yet the legacy of Sokolyansky and Meshcheryakov presents a research-based, differentiated system working within a strong and sophisticated philosophical and psychological framework, that is characteristic of the Soviet defectological system itself. It has the added attraction of pushing back the frontiers of knowledge about handicapped children and how they might be educated. For anyone wishing to 'get to grips' with the Soviet system of special teaching, the deaf-blind field is a most rewarding area for investigation.

The lack of attention from educators of the deaf-blind themselves is less easy to explain. Specialist libraries in Britain and the USA hold very little English-language (even less Russian) material on Soviet work, and occasional visits by professionals to Moscow and Zagorsk have resulted only in brief, sometimes misleading reports, with no follow-up in terms of increased contact and research. It has been left to professionals in Scandinavia and the Netherlands to take more meaningful interest and make some (if still very limited) use of Soviet expertise in their own approaches.

For educators of the deaf-blind and therefore for deaf-blind children themselves, the potential benefits of greater knowledge and contact are considerable. Despite official trends towards generalisation in special education, with often wholesale identification of the needs of deaf-blind children with those of the severely and profoundly handicapped, (36) specialised deaf-blind education in the West still clings to a belief in the unfulfilled potential of deaf-blind children and in the power of specialised teaching to make profound alterations to their developmental prospects. It is also clear that the pedagogy to make such 'transformations' on a regular basis is not part of the Western knowledge base. If the Soviet Union has such knowledge and is able to put it into practice on a regular basis, as evidenced by attainments at the Zagorsk Home, then we should be keen to share it. Much depends on the extent to which contact can be advanced - assimilating Soviet expertise is not likely to come about by taking books off shelves, but by capitalising on experience and co-operating in practice. At least from this point of view present developments are encouraging. If glasnost makes access by Westerners to Soviet defectological expertise easier one hopes that interested professionals will not be slow in examining and applying it - for the benefit of the deaf-blind everywhere.

NOTES

1.   S.D. Myers, 'A general overview of disabilities and handicaps,' in S.R. Walsh and R. Holzberg, Understanding the Deaf-Blind/Severely and Profoundly Handicapped (Charles C. Thomas, Springfield, 1981), pp. 4344.

2.   B. Maizel, 'Education of blind and deaf mutes in the USSR,' Teacher of the Deaf, 1947, vol. 45, no. 266, p. 52.

3.   A.I. Meshcheryakov, 'Pamyati Ivana Afanasievicha Sokolyanskovo,' in I.A. Sokolyansky, A.I. Meshcheryakov (eds), Obuchenie i vospitanie slepoglukhonemykh (Izdatelstvo Akademii pedagogicheskikh nauk RSFSR, Moscow, 1962), p. 5.

4.   O.I. Skorokhodova, Kak ya vosprinimayu,

predstavlyayu i ponimayu okruzhayushchy mir (Pedagogika, Moscow, 1972), p. 27.

5. G.P. Bertyn, I.D. Lukasheva, M.C. Pevzner, 'Proiskhozhdenie slozhnykh defektov u detei,' Prichiny vozniknoveniya i puti profilaktiki anomalii razvitiya u detei (Akademiya pedagogicheskikh nauk, Moscow, 1985), p. 66.

6. G.S. Gurgenidze, E.V. Ilenkov, 'Vydavushcheyesya dostizhenie sovetskoi nauki,' Voprosy filosofii, 1975, no. 6, p. 64.

7. See Sokolyansky, Meshcheryakov, Obuchenie i vospitanie.

8. A.I. Meshcheryakov, Slepoglukhonemye deti: razvitie psikhiki v protsesse formirovaniya povedeniya (Pedagogika, Moscow, 1974).

9. A.I. Meshcheryakov, Awakening to Life: Forming Behaviour and the Mind in Deaf-Blind Children (Progress Publishers, Moscow, 1974).

10. A.I. Meshcheryakov, 'Forming of image by the blind and deaf and dumb child, and the structure of image,' in Teaching Deaf-Blind Children. Report of a Seminar on the Teaching of Deaf-Blind Children, Condover Hall, 27-31 July 1962 (Royal National Institute for the Blind, London, 1962).

11. S. Sirotkin, 'Address to Committee on Services to the Deaf-Blind at the First Helen Keller World Conference, 11-16 September 1977,' in A Conference of Hope. Proceedings of the First Historic Helen Keller Conference (World Council for the Welfare of the Blind, New York, 1977).

12. V.N. Chulkov, 'Voprosy izucheniya psikhicheskovo razvitiya slepoglukhonemykh detei i kharakteristika variantov razvitiya pri slepoglukhote,' in Korrektsionno-vospitatelnaya rabota s detmi pri glubokikh narusheniyakh zreniya i slukha (Akademiya pedagogicheskikh nauk SSSR, Moscow, 1986).

13. A.I. Meshcheryakov, 'Initial teaching and development of the deaf and blind and mute child,' Blind Welfare: Southern Regional Review, no. 46 (1968), p. 2.

14. Meshcheryakov, Awakening to Life, p. 95.

15. Meshcheryakov, 'Initial teaching ...,' p. 5.

16. Meshcheryakov, Awakening to Life, p. 168.

17. Meshcheryakov, 'Initial teaching ...,' p. 7.

18. Meshcheryakov, 'Pamyati ...,' p. 7.

19. Meshcheryakov, Awakening to Life, pp. 122 and 124.

20. Ibid., p. 153.

Educating the Deaf-Blind*

Educating the Deaf-Blind

Educating the Deaf-Blind

Educating the Deaf-Blind

21. Ibid., p. 86.
22. A.V. Apraushev, Vospitanie optimizmom: Zapiski direktora zagorskovo detskovo doma dlya slepoglukhonemykh detei (Pedagogika, Moscow, 1983), p. 33.
23. Meshcheryakov, Awakening to Life, pp. 112-13.
24. R.A. Mareeva, Vospitanie i obuchenie slepoglukhonemyykh detei v semye (Vserossiyskoe obshchestvo slepykh, Moscow, 1979), pp. 62.
25. Ibid., p. 69.
26. A.I. Meshcheryakov, 'Peculiarities of mental development of the blind, deaf and dumb child in the process of elementary education,' in Problems of Mental Development and Social Psychology. Abstracts of Communications from the XVIII International Congress of Psychology (Izdatelstvo Moskovskovo Universiteta, Moscow, 1966), pp. 240-1.
27. Meshcheryakov, Awakening to Life, p. 68.
28. Meshcheryakov, 'Forming of image ...,' p. 62.
29. Meshcheryakov, Awakening to Life, p. 179.
30. Ibid., p. 303.
31. A. Avilova, V. Prut, 'Graduation day at Moscow University: deaf-blind students receive degrees in psychology,' Rehabilitation/WORLD, vol. 3, no. 4 (1977-78), p. 12.
32. Quoted in K. Watkins, 'Report on the Institute of Defectology, Moscow USSR,' in Theories into Practice. Proceedings of the Fifth International Deaf-Blind Seminar, held at Condover Hall, 26 July - 1 August 1974 (RNIB and International Council for the Visually Handicapped, London, 1974), p. 30.
33. Meshcheryakov, Awakening to Life, p. 291.
34. Ibid., p. 30.
35. Ibid., p. 84.
36. M.D. Orlansky, 'The deaf-blind and the severely/profoundly handicapped: an emerging relationship,' in S.R. Walsh, R. Holzberg, Understanding the Deaf-Blind/Severely and Profoundly Handicapped (Charles C. Thomas, Springfield, 1981), pp. 5-24.

Chapter Six

CHILDREN WITH LEARNING DIFFICULTIES

Avril Suddaby

INTRODUCTION

Children with learning difficulties in the Soviet Union are to be found in both ordinary and special schools. In 1982 the population of special schools was about half a million. Special schools provide for children with all types of disabilities but the largest single group of special schools is the auxiliary schools (vspomogatelnye shkoly) for children who are intellectually impaired or mentally retarded. The half a million in special schools represent a tiny proportion (a little more than 1%) of the school-age population; there must therefore be many children with learning difficulties for whose education the mass schools take responsibility. Defining slow learners is problematical and numbers vary according to definitions used. In most British studies, some 15% is generally accepted as representing slow learners in the school population. (1)

Because Soviet mass schools operate with a compulsory common curriculum, which appears more suitable for academic children than for slow learners, it is instructive to see how the educational problem of less academic pupils is tackled. As there is no streaming in Soviet schools it is also difficult to identify slow learners amongst the pupils of the mass school, especially as grade repeating, at one time a convenient way of identifying children with learning difficulties, seems to have been almost eliminated. The numbers of grade repeaters used to be high (10% of all primary schoolchildren in the 1950s), by the 1970s the problem had been virtually eliminated and less than half of 1% of children were then repeating a grade. According to

Vestnik statistiki, 'In the 1984-85 school year some 204,000 pupils (0.5% of all pupils) were repeating a grade.' (2)

With the continuing differentiation that has been taking place recently in Soviet education, slightly more children with learning difficulties are now likely to be educated in the special school system than was the case just a few years previously. This chapter aims to describe the new provision for children with learning difficulties and to look at other recent developments which affect the education of slow learners. First, we show the basis of selection of children for special education in order to explain the distinction, from the Soviet viewpoint, between those who should be in special schools and those who are more suited to education in the mass schools. Second, in regard to the increasing differentiation which has been taking place recently in Soviet education, we outline the slight shift in this traditional distinction between children who should and should not have special education. We describe the research which took place in the 1970s and brought about this change. Third, our focus will be on the educational provision for slow learners in Moscow. Finally, we mention the most recent developments affecting slow learning pupils.

SELECTION OF CHILDREN FOR AUXILIARY SCHOOLS

Most of the children who are educated in auxiliary schools are oligophrenic, i.e. they have incurred brain damage which makes learning impossible in ordinary educational conditions. Selection of oligophrenic children for the auxiliary school is carried out by medical-educational commissions (mediko-pedagogicheskie kommissii). (3) Children are referred to the commission either by their teachers if they are having difficulty in the ordinary school, or by the day nursery they have attended, or by the local polyclinic.

The commission is multidisciplinary and comprises a speech therapist, a psychoneurologist and a defectologist. The principle on which diagnosis of oligophrenia is based is that of damage to the central nervous system (CNS) which prevents the child from learning successfully under ordinary conditions. The damage will have occurred at either the interuterine stage, at birth, or possibly as a result of an early childhood illness. CNS damage which occurs later in life would not be accepted for a diagnosis of oligophrenia because secondary mental function would have had time to

141

develop and, with the plasticity of the human organism, these developed mental functions should be able to compensate for damaged functions. However, if damage occurs early in life before important secondary functions have had time to develop, subsequent development is bound to be anomalous and special education is required to put it back on the right course as far as may be possible.

The concept of oligophrenia is therefore in part physiologically based. Simple failure to make progress at school might be the cause of the child's referral to the medical-educational commission; but mere failure to make educational progress is not in itself sufficient for a diagnosis of oligophrenia. The commission's examination of the child includes a comprehensive study of the mother's health during pregnancy, the circumstances of the birth and the child's developmental history. EEGs, an investigation of the child's HNA (higher nervous activity) and a full medical examination are also standard procedure.

Of equal importance in the medical diagnosis carried out by the commission is evaluation of the child's ability to learn. This is done by means of a 'test' which is very different from standardised tests used in the West. The concept of the Zone of Next Development, developed by L.S. Vygotsky, is the basis of Soviet tests (see Chapter 3). The child is set a problem which is too difficult to solve without help, i.e. it is within the next, not the present zone of development. (4) Next the child is given help and again tackles the same or a similar test. An evaluation is then made of ability to learn based on the amount and nature of the help required, and the child's ability to transfer what it has learned in an analogous task; that is, to generalise. A brain-damaged child who shows very little ability to make progress and generalise what it has learned even with adult help would be classified as oligophrenic and sent to a special school.

INCREASING DIFFERENTIATION

In the past, borderline cases were described simply as 'pseudo-oligophrenic' and would have been returned to the normal school to continue education. (5) Such children must have been - and still are - a major problem in large classes in the mass schools where the curriculum is demanding and compulsory for all subjects. In recent years, however, the concept of temporary delay in mental development (vremennaya zaderzhka psikhicheskovo razvitiya) has had growing attention.

There are some problems in translating the concept of zaderzhka psikhicheskovo razvitiya (usually abbreviated to ZPR). In Russian the words 'um' (mind or intellect) and 'psikhika' (psyche) are both in current use with their corresponding adjectives. 'Psikhika' is a much broader term, encompassing both emotional and intellectual development. The notion umstvennaya otstalost is conventionally translated as intellectual impairment, mental handicap and also sometimes as mental retardation, the latter sounding little different from 'delay in mental development'. The literal translation of ZPR, 'delay in psychic development', is almost meaningless in English because historically the word 'psychic' has connotations with the supernatural. For that reason, the potentially misleading 'delay in mental development' is used in translation. It is essential to bear in mind that this is qualitatively different from intellectual impairment/mental handicap/mental retardation (umstvennaya ostalost).

Since definitions and perceptions differ in other countries, it is as well to give here a fairly lengthy definition. The 1970 edition of the Dictionary of Defectology offers the following definition of zaderzhka psikhicheskovo razvitiya (delay in mental development):

A disturbance in the normal rate of mental development, as a result of which the child, on attaining school age, continues to remain under the influence of pre-school and of play interests. With a delay in mental development children are unable to participate in school activity, to begin and complete school tasks. They behave in class as though they were in a play group in a day nursery or at home. Children with temporary ZPR are often erroneously considered to be intellectually impaired ... The difference between these two groups involves two characteristics. Although children with ZPR have difficulty in mastering elementary reading, writing and arithmetic skills, this is combined with a relatively weakly-developed language ability, considerably higher aptitudes for remembering verse and stories, and a higher level of development of cognitive activity. This combination is not characteristic of the intellectually impaired. Furthermore children with temporary ZPR are invariably able to take advantage of help given them while they are working, mastering the principle of task-solution, and transferring this principle to the execution of another, similar task. This shows that they possess the full capacity for further development, i.e. they will subsequently be able to execute independently that which, in the special instructional situation, they are presently able to complete only with the teacher's assistance. Prolonged observations of children with ZPR have shown that it is precisely this ability to utilise assistance when it is offered and to apply their learning intelligently in the process of future instruction that results in their eventually being able to learn successfully in the mass school. (6)

RESEARCH INTO ZPR IN THE 1970s

From the mid-seventies close attention was paid to children who were not oligophrenic but who were having difficulty with their schoolwork. Classes, and then schools, were established on an experimental basis to investigate children with a delay in mental development (ZPR). This research work was conducted by psychologists at the General Psychology and Education Research Institute attached to the Academy of Pedagogical Sciences. At the same time, the Institute of Defectology began investigating clinical problems of temporary delay in mental development. (7)

Zoya Kalmykova of the General Psychology and Education Institute, a leading researcher in this field, investigated the types of thinking used in problem-solving. She found that children with the greatest ability in problem-solving had mastered what she called abstract-theoretical thinking; less able primary grade (7-11) children, and especially children with a temporary delay in mental development (ZPR), were not capable of this type of thinking and used a type of thinking which relied on concrete illustrations and practical actions, described as 'visual-operational' thinking. (8)

In general it was found that children with temporary ZPR could learn, but they learned more slowly than most children and also required special teaching methods which took into consideration their dominant mode of thinking. For some time it was debated whether it was best to establish separate classes in ordinary schools for such children or to educate them in separate establishments. In fact, separate education for children with ZPR was tested in experimental schools and classes during the 1970s; then in 1981 the USSR Ministry of Education published Regulations giving guidance and direction for the operation of schools for children with a temporary delay in mental development. (9) The experimental schools became official and ZPR schools became a regular feature of Soviet special education provision.

THE 1981 REGULATIONS

The Regulations state that the new type of special schools can operate either as boarding schools or as extended day schools. They admit 7-9 year olds; either children who 'have persistent difficulty in mastering the learning material' from grades 1 and 2 of the mass school or potential school starters who 'are not prepared for mastery of school subjects.' (10)

The Regulations are precise and detailed and specify the curriculum and examinations to be used, the numbers of pupils to be enrolled in the schools and class sizes, the staffing, financing and equipping of the schools, the pupils to be admitted and the rules governing transfer from and to the mass schools.

In general the Regulations ensure that ideal conditions are provided in which the children's delay in mental development can be corrected. One speech therapist (logoped) is provided for every 25-30 children with speech problems. Teachers and upbringers must be trained defectologists who have 'to deal with special tasks to correct deficiencies in the children's mental development, in addition to the normal tasks laid down by the General Secondary School Regulations.' (11)

Like teachers in auxiliary schools, teachers in ZPR schools are paid 20 per cent above normal salary. Classes comprise not more than 20 children; a daytime nap is compulsory for primary grades and for some senior grade children if this is recommended by doctors. The Regulations stipulate that in all grades part of lesson time should be given to physical exercise.

The standard timetable of the mass schools is used, including labour training, although it does dispense with some Russian language lessons. (12) The principle of the timetable is to allow extra time to cover the standard eight-year programme of the normal school. This extra time is provided in the form of an additional year in which to complete the three (or now four) primary grades; the additional year can be either before starting grade 1 for children who have not yet started school, or as an extra year on completion of the primary grades for children who are transferred from the mass schools.

Other than this extra-time allowance for completing the programme, no concessions are made: the full range of subjects is taken, including a non-Soviet foreign language. For non-Russian speaking children Russian would be taught as well as a foreign language.

The reason for using the curriculum of the mass school is that the aim of the ZPR school is to correct the delay in development and to return the child to mainstream education. After completion of the primary grades each child is re-assessed by the Education Council to see if he or she is capable of continuing education in the normal school. Only the most severe cases of ZPR stay in the special school for the duration of their education. According to early reports, the average return to normal education is 40% for the entire USSR. (13)

Judging by the Regulations, the concept of ZPR is, like that of oligophrenia, physiologically based; the primary cause of the retardation is described as follows: 'a delay in psychic development of a cerebral-organic origin - usually of a residual nature - as a result of infection, trauma or intoxication of the nervous system, more rarely a result of genetically-conditioned handicaps to development.' (14) The ZPR takes the form of defects in memory, concentration, speed of mental processes in the cognitive sphere and a reduced level of performance, and it is connected with a minimal underdevelopment of some cerebral cortical functions.

Significance of the new developments

How should this new development in Soviet special education be interpreted? Does it represent a fundamental change in traditional Soviet attitudes to special education needs? The West Germany-based comparativist Leonid Novikov has no doubt that 'at the start of the 1980s the psychosomatic illnesses affecting children and the distinct forms of infantilism needing cure and remedial treatment have made their way into the Soviet educational system.' (15) Novikov reaches this conclusion by focusing on a clause in the 1981 Regulations which states that in exceptional cases the following clinical variations of ZPR can be admitted to the new type of school:

'(a) constitutional (harmonic), mental and psychophysical infantilism.
(b) ZPR of somatogenic origin accompanied by forms of persistent somatic asthenia and somatically conditioned infantilism.
(c) ZPR of psychogenic origin following pathological personality development of a neurotic type, accompanied by signs of mental inertia and psychogenic infantilism.' (16)

If ZPR schools become widespread, the exceptional cases of children with personality problems might increasingly be accommodated in them. However, while such schools are at present rare it is most likely that their intake will be those children specified in the Regulations who have CNS damage which is not sufficiently severe and permanent to warrant a diagnosis of oligophrenia. In other words, there has been a slight broadening of the concept of need for special education; but no fundamental change has taken place.

Novikov's attitude to the Regulations is ambiguous. He sees them as permitting the mass school to get rid of its problem pupils, those suffering from what is termed 'pedagogic neglect'. Yet he also welcomes this new development as it follows what he describes as years of stagnation in Soviet defectology in which there was virtually no real structural or quantitative development.

Whether or not one approves of the physiological basis of the Soviet definition of mental handicap, the accusation that there has been virtually no real structural or quantitative development is certainly unfounded. Increasing refinement of the categories of special education has been a feature of Soviet special education over the years, and quantitatively the numbers in special education are little different from those in Western countries. There is a danger that children suffering from pedagogic neglect could be wrongly placed in the ZPR school, inasmuch as an exceptional category is children with pathological personality development ('ZPR of psychogenic origin following pathological personality development of a neurotic type'). There is, nonetheless, a significant difference between inadequate character development implied by pedagogic neglect and the pathological personality development envisaged in the Regulations.

Novikov expresses the hope that in future the increase in opportunities for Soviet special schooling will be determined solely by humane considerations, as ideological constraints have, he feels, restricted its development in the past. It is clear that Marxist philosophy has influenced Soviet special education, but it is arguable whether this has resulted in a provision of special education which is either quantitatively or qualitatively inferior to that of other industrialised nations.

ROLE OF THE INSTITUTE OF DEFECTOLOGY

With the establishment of the new type of special schools, the centre for research into ZPR has shifted from the Psychology and Education Institute to the Institute of Defectology. What had been previously primarily a psychopedagogical problem has become chiefly a clinical one. A laboratory has been established under the leadership of Professor V.I. Lubovsky at the Institute of Defectology to conduct research into ZPR, and a growing number of publications about ZPR have appeared in the 1980s in the Institute's journal, Defektologiya, many of them on differential diagnosis of ZPR.

Since the move of ZPR research to the Institute of Defectology the word 'temporary' has been virtually dropped from 'temporary delay in mental development'. The emphasis has therefore shifted subtly from a transitory educational problem to be mastered in the pedagogic process to a clinical problem that may require long-term special educational help and so is analogous to other defectological conditions.

As this is an especially sensitive and problematic area of diagnosis, the Medical Educational Commission at the Institute of Defectology deals with all cases of suspected ZPR in Moscow to decide which children should attend Moscow School No 23 for ZPR Children, which had been in the 1970s the Institute's experimental school in this field and it remains Moscow's sole ZPR school. In diagnosis the concept of Zone of Next Development continues to play a major role in distinguishing ZPR from oligophrenia. Also of great importance is investigation into the predominant mode of thinking (Kalmykova's 'visual-operational mode of thinking'). Despite the extensive research into differential diagnosis, no clear indicators have yet emerged to differentiate ZPR clearly from closely-related conditions by use of EEGs, etc. The main criterion in diagnosis still appears to be evaluation of the child's potential by measuring its Zone of Next Development and assessment of the predominant mode of thinking. (17)

THE MOSCOW ZPR SCHOOL

In many ways Moscow School No 23 for ZPR Children is very like the auxiliary schools. (18) It has the same small classes as in the auxiliary school and, as usual, boys outnumber girls. The same concern is shown for the children's physical care and the curative regime. There are extensive medical facilities and a large staff of medical personnel: doctors, nurses, a dentist, speech therapist and physiotherapist. Like most auxiliary schools, it is a boarding school, although most pupils go home at weekends. The School has on staff several 'upbringers' (vospitateli) and much emphasis is put on 'upbringing work' (vospitanie) to develop the children's moral and social education.

In so far as the standard mass-school curriculum is used, the School is closer to an ordinary mass school than to a special school. All children take the full range of subjects of the ordinary school, including a non-Soviet foreign language. (How many Western slow learners continue with a foreign language, or physics, for the full extent of their schooling?) An extra year is allowed to cover the four primary grades and to make up for the children's delay in mental development. Once a school start at age six becomes standard for all children in the USSR, five years will be allowed to complete the primary grades, but so far (1987) only about 30% of Moscow schoolchildren start school when they are six. (19)

One surprising feature of the Moscow ZPR school is that the children do their labour lessons (woodwork/metalwork) only in the school, and do not go out to a local factory (as appears to be the case in most auxiliary schools). With the greater emphasis on manual work since the 1984 educational reforms, it seems strange that in a school which is so close in many ways to normal educational provision, the usual system of patronage (shefstvo) of a local enterprise is not used. Although manual work is by no means neglected - the school has well-equipped carpentry and metalwork workshops - the emphasis seems to be firmly on children's mental development.

On completion of grade three (age nine) all children are examined by the Medical-Educational Commission to see if they are capable of continuing their education in the ordinary school. Approximately 50% are transferred on completion of the primary grades to ordinary schools, where their progress is monitored for one year. According to the Moscow ZPR School head, about 50% proceed to normal education after completing their course in School. If so, this compares favourably with the 40% return rate for the whole of the USSR from ZPR schools. The remaining children complete their education in the special ZPR school. The matriculation lists of children who stay on at the ZPR school show most of the children continuing with their further education at technical colleges (PTUs), evening institutes, or the top two grades of the mass school. There are even reports of graduates of ZPR schools eventually going on to higher education.

NEW DEVELOPMENTS

It might be expected that, with the demanding curriculum of normal schools which is taxing for many children, there would be an increase in the number of schools for ZPR children. Surprisingly this does not seem to be happening. Only 34 were reported to exist in the country in 1983; and in Moscow with some 10 million inhabitants there is still only the one ZPR school. (20) On the other hand, the small Transcaucasian Republic of Armenia (19) with only 4.5 million people possesses three ZPR schools. Instead of more ZPR schools, another form of 'remedial' education has appeared in Moscow schools. This takes the form of catching-up classes (klassy vyravnivaniya) in the normal schools, an experiment which first started in the Baltic Republics. (21) Teachers of such classes have to be qualified defectologists and receive the same 20% salary increment as do their colleagues in special educational schools.

No new legislation would have been necessary to govern

the opening and operation of the levelling-up classes as they appear to be covered by a clause in the above-mentioned 1981 Regulations. This clause also allows for the provision of day attendance by ZPR pupils, while making clear that boarding conditions are to be the norm: 'Extended-day groups for day pupils may operate in the special boarding schools for children with delay in mental development. In exceptional cases and with the agreement of the Republican ministries of education, special classes for ZPR children may exist among extended-day groups in the general schools.' (22)

Professor Lubovsky of the Institute of Defectology has told the author that although about 5% of children suffer from ZPR, not all of the 5% need special education. In his view, only about 2% need special education, and the new special classes in the mass schools are appropriate for the remainder.

Many Soviet educationists seem to view the catching-up classes with some dismay. They feel that ordinary schools do not possess ideal conditions for correcting children's anomalous development, whereas they are provided in ZPR schools. Some educationists see them as the 'thin end of the wedge' in that they could lead to undesirable stratification in Soviet schools if such classes spread and are used by teachers as 'dumping grounds' for their problem pupils.

Another recent arrival in Soviet education - the school psychological services - is doubtless intended to play a part in advising on the correctional treatment of backward pupils in ordinary schools. (23) Again, this development is one which has not met with universal approval. Ever since the 1936 Decree on Pedological Perversions, Soviet education has shunned standardised tests, such as are used by Western psychologists. (24) The concern is that such tests, generally seen as at best useless and more often as harmful, are being reintroduced. However, this experiment is still on too small a scale for any definite conclusions to be reached.

It is not yet clear on exactly what basis pupils are being selected for catching-up classes. If it is purely on the basis of lack of achievement, such classes will inevitably contain what are known as 'pedagogically neglected' pupils, a group which the Soviet special school system has so far taken pains to exclude. In the case of pedagogic neglect, since the pupil is regarded as intellectually and physically sound, there is no apparent reason for her or him not to do well; yet educational failure still occurs. Such a child may

151

suddenly stop trying at school; initially, schoolwork may have been too easy and the pupil failed to respond to the challenge of increasingly difficult work. Or the pupil's parents may have spoilt him, so that correct attitudes to work failed to develop. In such cases the problem has traditionally been one which the pupil and the ordinary schoolteacher had to solve.

OVERVIEW

The Soviet approach to special and remedial education offers interesting contrasts to Western approaches. In Britain, at least since the Warnock Report, there have been moves to integrate handicapped children into mainstream education wherever possible. Also, since Warnock, the different categories of handicap have been replaced by the single term 'special educational needs'. The aim is the admirable one of treating the handicapped with respect and of integrating them into society, thereby breaking down what are seen as largely artificial barriers.

The Soviet approach is generally to identify the nature of the handicap and to provide an education which offers the best way of compensating for that handicap. The 'best' way, from the Soviet point of view, involves segregated education, inasmuch as a specialised institution can provide the specialist equipment and staff needed to deal with the particular disability. Certainly, Soviet special schools have staffing ratios and facilities which would be the envy of British special educationists (see Chapter 3).

The principle of the Soviet curriculum for the handicapped is that of following the standard timetable of ordinary schools as closely as possible. In schools for the deaf and hard of hearing, for example, the standard curriculum is followed, while additional time is allowed for the children to complete the programmes. On the other hand, the mentally-handicapped deaf and hard of hearing follow the curriculum of the auxiliary schools for mentally handicapped pupils; their education takes place either in separate specialised institutions for this type of child or in separate classes in a special school for the deaf and hard of hearing. (25)

In the case of slow learners, i.e. the less able, rather than the severely handicapped, children, the traditional British approach is to provide adaptive, corrective or remedial education. The strategies vary according to the educational stage. At the primary stage, although slow learners are sometimes withdrawn from normal lessons for special remedial classes, most children are taught together for at least most of the time. At the secondary stage, the differences between slow learners and their peers become more obvious and it is more common for separate teaching to be provided; in over 60% of secondary schools investigated for the Schools Council Report in 1979, there were separate teaching arrangements for the 15-20% of children identified as slow learners. Also, as the title of the Schools Council Report - Curricular Needs of Slow Learners - indicates, slow learners are seen as in need of a different curriculum from their 'normal' peers. (26)

Although British children are therefore physically integrated by all being in the same geographical location, they are divided within schools by the curriculum. This curricular segregation is seen by most teachers of slow learners as being in their pupils' best interests, but it has troubled some educationists. As one teacher has written, 'If the objectives of our education differ for some pupils, either because they are considered too difficult, or for some reason they are thought less important for these pupils, then ... we have indeed got inequality of educational opportunity of the most far-reaching kind.' (27) The notion that teachers are actually depriving their pupils of equality of opportunity must be a disturbing one for many teachers of slow learners.

The Soviet approach is to offer the same curricular opportunities for all, and to give additional assistance where needed; in the case of some pupils, extra time is allowed to cover the standard curriculum. Such pupils are seen as slow learners who take longer than average to cover their work rather than as non-learners who would never manage to cover the curriculum. The British approach tends to provide a curriculum which is relevant and appropriate to the child rather than one which might cause unhappiness by making unrealistic if not impossible demands on the child.

Soviet 'defectologists' have obtained remarkable results in their ZPR schools. If the same results are going to be achieved by the ZPR classes and if they are eventually established in all Soviet schools, can the problem of slow learners be considered solved? That remains to be seen, but it offers exciting prospects. The question of which approach leads to greater human happiness is impossible to answer since it is not readily measurable. It may be that the British slow learner has a more relaxed childhood, but what happens once schooldays are over and the world of work begins? In the competitive British job market, the slow learner, deprived of an opportunity of obtaining the valued certificates that employers require, stands little chance of finding employment beyond a short-term youth-training scheme. The Soviet slow learner leaves school equipped with the same certificate of secondary education as his or her peers and has, at least in theory, the same opportunities for finding the sort of employment which she or he wishes to take up.

To Western educationists accustomed to easier curricula and separate teaching arrangements for slow learners, the Soviet approach might seem so demanding of less able children as to be described as harsh. Yet if the purpose of education is the maximum development of intellectual potential, the Soviet example has much to recommend it. Similarly, to those Western educationists concerned with liberal ideas of integrating those who are different into mainstream education, the Soviet approach to handicapped pupils will seem retrogressive and even demeaning to the handicapped. In Soviet eyes an education system that expects the handicapped child to cope in the same educational conditions as normal children is to be condemned.

Both the British and Soviet education systems aim to integrate handicapped children into normal society. In the USSR this is done by giving the handicapped person a vocational training so that he or she can eventually take part in society's productive effort. The aim of integration is viewed within the context of the ZPR school where the backward child has to follow the standard curriculum, thereby giving the pupil the chance to transfer to normal education at some stage. To Westerners used to permitting children to drop 'difficult' subjects, the Soviet approach may seem rather inflexible. And there can be no doubt that great demands are made on ZPR children since even normal children find the Soviet curriculum taxing. However, an education system that strives for the maximum development of individual potential and provides the staff and facilities to try to achieve this is certainly deserving of respect for its aims as well as its achievements.

NOTES

1.   See Schools Council Working Paper 63 (London, 1979) which uses a definition of the 15-20% of pupils making the least satisfactory progress with their schoolwork. A survey by HM Inspectorate (Department of Education and Science, London, 1971) identified 14% of pupils as slow learners.
2.   Vestnik statistiki, no. 8 (1986), p. 71.
3.   T.A. Vlasova, K.S. Lebedinskaya, V.F. Machikhina, Otbor detei vo vspomogatelnuyu shkolu (Prosveshchenie, Moscow, 1983).
4.   See L.S. Vygotsky, Sobranie sochinenii, vol. 2, (Pedagogika, Moscow, 1982), pp. 246-8.
5.   See A. Sutton, 'Backward children in the USSR,' in J. Brine, M. Perrie, A. Sutton (eds), Home, School and Leisure in the Soviet Union (Allen and Unwin, London, 1980), p. 176.
6.   A.I. Dyachkov, Defektologichesky slovar (Prosveshchenie, Moscow, 1964), p. 81.
7.   The earliest report of collaborative research on ZPR by the Institute of Defectology and the Institute of General Psychology and Education is that of T.A. Vlasova, M.S. Pevsner (eds), Deti s vremennimi zaderzhkami razvitiya (Pedagogika, Moscow, 1971).
8.   See Z.I. Kalmykova, Produktivnoe myshlenie kak osnova obuchaemosti (Pedagogika, Moscow, 1981). A brief account of this work is contained in Defektologiya, no. 3 (1978), pp. 3-8.
9.   See 'Tipovoye polozhenie o spetsialnoi obshcheobrazovatelnoi shkole-internate (shkola s prod-lyonnym dnyom) dlya detei s zaderzhkoi psikhicheskovo razvitiya,' Byulleten normativnikh aktov Ministerstva prosveshcheniya SSSR (Moscow, 1982), pp. 26-38.
10.   Ibid., p. 27.
11.   Ibid., p. 34.
12.   See P. Stringer, 'Special education in the Soviet Union and the child with learning difficulties,' Association of Educational Psychologists Journal, vol. 6, no. 4 (1984), pp. 2-18. Stringer gives an account of a 'special lesson' whose purpose was to link up the child's various other lessons.
13.   See 'O predvaritelnykh rezultatakh obucheniya i vospitaniya detei s zaderzhkoi psikhicheskovo razvitiya v spetsialnykh shkolakh i klassakh,' Byulleten normativnykh aktov Ministerstva prosveshcheniya SSSR (Moscow, 1983),

no. 6, pp. 23-4.
    14.   Ibid., p. 27.
    15.   L. Novikov, 'Some aspects of the development of special education in the Soviet Union,' in J. Tomiak (ed.), Western Perpsectives on Soviet Education in the 1980s (Macmillan, London, 1986), pp. 191-207.
    16.   'Tipovoye polozhenie o spetsialnoi ...,' p. 28.
    17.   Communication at the Defectology Faculty of Moscow's Lenin Pedagogical Institute in October 1986.
    18.   Reports of visits by the author of this chapter to Moscow School No. 23 appeared in the Times Educational Supplement, 22 June 1984, p. 20, and in Special Children, no. 8, February 1987, pp. 22-3.
    19.   Communication from School No. 23 Head, Iosif Averbuch.
    20.   See Stringer.
    21.   Z.I. Kalmykova, Psikhologicheskie printsipy razvivayushchevo obucheniya (Znanie, Moscow, 1979), p. 39.
    22.   Ibid., p. 30.
    23.   I.V. Dubrovina, 'Psikhologicheskaya sluzhba v shkole,' Sovetskaya pedagogika, no. 1 (1986), pp. 46-50.
    24.   See A. Sutton, in Brine, Perrie, Sutton, Home, School and Leisure, p. 164.
    25.   See G.D. Kuznetsov (ed.), V pomoshch direktoru spetsialnoi shkoly (Prosveshchenie, Moscow, 1982).
    26.   See Schools Council Working Paper 63: Curricular Needs of Slow Learners (Evans/Methuen, London, 1979).
    27.   P.H. Hirst, 'The logic of the curriculum,' Journal of Curriculum Studies, vol. 1, no. 2 (1969), pp. 157-8.

Chapter Seven

A PROFILE OF STUDENTS IN HIGHER EDUCATION

George Avis

INTRODUCTION

The student is the central figure in the perestroika (of
higher education). He is the focus of our main concern
because only a few years are allotted to give to the
former school pupil, worker, collective farmer and
soldier the knowledge and skills to enable them to enter
the workshop as a commander of production or the
operation theatre as a surgeon or the classroom as a
teacher. Everything that is done in college and
university - lectures, seminars, private study, all plans,
ideas and upbringing - must be subordinated to this
task.

(Pravda leader, 29 April 1987)

Students in Soviet VUZs (higher education establishments),
(1) though they may not all be described as gifted, are
certainly a select group. They constitute an intellectual
elite from which the future leaders and organisers of
economic, political and cultural life are drawn. In the long
term the success of socialism and the advent of communism
depend upon them. And in the medium term Mikhail
Gorbachov is relying on them to help implement his
programme of radical restructuring of Soviet life, including
the system of higher education. It is not, therefore,
surprising that students as future graduate specialists have
received a great deal of attention in the media from the
government and Party. They represent, after all, the crucial
'human factor' in graduate labour resource planning. But
current expressions of concern and exhortations differ from

157

those of the past in that now under Gorbachov's perestroika students really are to be given more independence, more time to think for themselves and be creative, and more control over their life and work. (2)

Our aim in this chapter is a limited one, namely to examine, albeit briefly, the main characteristics of Soviet students today and of their academic work. In so doing we shall touch upon some of the problems which affect Soviet higher education in general, the sort of problems, indeed, which have led to current proposals for major reform in the tertiary system. Of necessity, what follows is a rather selective treatment and important aspects of student life are sometimes merely referred to in passing or neglected entirely.

For our sources we rely mainly on Soviet statistical and survey data, official documents and the educational press. There are serious faults and gaps in this sort of evidence, as most students of Soviet studies are aware. Even the most basic statistical information is simply not made available by the relevant Soviet authorities. (3) For example, publication of results of the last (1979) Census has been restricted to just one slim volume. And this omits age-group data crucial for the study of young people. No official statistics have been issued by the Ministry of Higher and Secondary Specialised Education since the late 1970s on the social composition of students or their attainment and wastage rates. And those which exist for earlier years frequently suffer from annoying imprecision. Similarly, sociological surveys carried out among students are rarely designed to yield results which are properly representative of the student body nationally. Nevertheless, in their accumulation and comparison such materials do help to identify general trends and to support experiential evidence.

STRUCTURE OF HIGHER EDUCATION

Before looking at student characteristics we should say something about the institutional structures and arrangements within which students have to live and work. As our opening quotation makes clear, the higher education system is unashamedly vocational in character. It sets out to produce a planned number of graduate specialists in designated fields to meet the centrally-determined needs of the economy. When young people enter higher education, therefore, they take on a four-, five- or six-year training course for a specific job, and they follow it in specialised institutes. When they graduate they are sent to work for an obligatory period of three years in factories, schools, farms and so on. Virtually all of the 896 higher education establishments in the Soviet Union are really specialised vocational institutes. The exception are some 69 universities, which teach a wide range of humanities, social sciences and pure natural sciences. But even they perform a particular vocational function, namely that of training future teachers and researchers. Of course, Soviet VUZs aim, too, to produce graduates with the right views and particular skills and qualities to make them leaders in their future work collectives - in other words, what Leonid Brezhnev described as 'politically literate and ideologically convinced fighters for the cause of communism'.

The scale of the operation is immense and involves huge numbers of students (see Table 7.1). The majority of the total five-million-plus student body are full-time day students. For this form of higher education an upper age limit of 35 is applied to entrants, but not for part-time courses. An increase in the proportion of part-time students in recent years has been prompted by the need to maintain an adequate output of graduate specialists despite a decline in the size of the relevant age group. At any given time about two million, or 40 per cent of all students, are in institutes which cater for industry and construction. Another one and a half million, or 30 per cent, are being trained as teachers. Nearly 590,000 of the latter are university students. 530,000 are destined to work in the agricultural sector, and another 376,000 will eventually work in medicine, the health services and physical education. (4)

At the All-Union level a USSR Ministry of Higher Education and Secondary Specialised Education has hitherto exercised overall responsibility. But many specialised VUZs come under the aegis of the particular economic ministries whose industries they supply with graduate specialists. This system of dual control is repeated in a second lower tier of government where 15 sets of Republican ministries are involved. Table 7.2 gives figures showing the number of students in each Republic per 10,000 of the population - a conventional mode of presentation - in order to illustrate the spread of higher education provision regionally over the last decade and a half. The figures record clear imbalances

Table 7.1: Numbers of students in Soviet higher education, 1970-1985

Total numbers	All (thousands)	%	Day (thousands)	%	Correspondence (thousands)	%	Evening (thousands)	%
1970	4,581	100	2,241	49	1,682	37	658	14
1975	4,854	100	2,628	54	1,582	33	644	13
1980	5,235	100	2,978	57	1,608	31	649	12
1985	5,147	100	2,763	54	1,750	34	634	12

Source: Narodnoe khozyaistvo SSSR v 1985 g. (Finansy i statistika, Moscow, 1986), p. 505

Table 7.2: Number of students per 10,000 inhabitants by Union Republic, 1970-1986

	1970-71	1975-76	1979-80	1985-86	%
USSR	188	190	196	185	100
Russian Federation	204	212	219	206	111
Belorussia	154	170	181	182	98
Lithuania	180	188	205	181	98
Kazakhstan	151	152	169	171	92
Georgia	189	168	170	169	91
Latvia	171	182	188	167	90
Ukraine	170	169	175	167	90
Armenia	214	190	187	163	88
Azerbaidzhan	191	173	172	158	85
Uzbekistan	192	174	173	154	83
Estonia	161	163	172	153	83
Kirgizia	162	151	154	144	78
Moldavia	124	115	127	128	69
Turkmenia	131	122	121	119	64
Tadzhikistan	149	144	141	118	64

Source: Narodnoe khozyaistvo SSSR v 1985 g. (Finansy i statistika, Moscow, 1986), p. 511.

and changes over the period. But two points must be underlined: (i) that the population of even the worst-served Republic enjoys superior provision than many advanced Western countries, and (ii) that in structure and content higher education is much the same throughout the huge federation which we know as the Soviet Union. So, if a Russian student from the Leningrad Polytechnic enters the portals of the polytechnic in Makhachkala in Dagestan or in Alma-Ata in Kazakhstan, he or she will find the academic process in both those places perfectly familiar. However, split jurisdiction does result in considerable duplication, faulty manpower planning, wasted effort and resources, not to mention horrendous bureaucracy.

STUDENT SELECTION

The first respect in which student youth differs from other

young people in the Soviet Union is that the former have successfully resisted the temptation of following alternative training channels open to them earlier on. At the age of fifteen, for example, after eight (now nine) grades of general schooling they have the opportunity to transfer to a vocational-technical school for manual trade training or to a technical college (<u>tekhnikum</u>) to qualify as a technician or medium-level nonmanual worker. It has been estimated that in 1982 some 38 per cent of their classmates did just that. And of those who stayed on in the general school over 50 per cent similarly moved on to this sort of vocational establishment later on when they had completed the tenth grade. Then again, they might have simply left school to take up employment as another third of tenth-graders did. But, in fact, they survived all these diversions to end up in the small minority of 15 per cent of schoolleavers who actually obtained a place in higher education. (5) In the following year, 1983, only 11 per cent of secondary school graduates obtained places in higher education. (6) Even after leaving school candidates for higher education have to go through what for many is a fairly stressful competitive entrance examination in one of their local VUZs (students usually do go to their nearest VUZs). If they fail to gain a place in their first choice of institution there is normally no opportunity to try elsewhere for a full-time place, so they have to wait for another year for a further attempt.

It must be said that nowadays the pressure of entry procedures is less than it used to be a decade or two ago simply because competition for places has slumped in recent years. (7) Many factors underlie this trend, but it is nevertheless rather surprising when one considers that so many more Soviet children now receive a full secondary general education. The swing from higher education in the seventies has resulted in an overall ratio of applications to places of less than two to one. (8) There are differences in demand between subjects, that is between types of institute. Competition for places in technological and agricultural institutes is lower than in most others and sometimes non-existent. Engineering which used to enjoy immense prestige among Soviet youth has now lost some of its popularity. Even the 'Imperial College' of the Soviet Union, the famous Bauman Institute in Moscow, has had trouble in meeting its intake targets. In medicine and the humanities, on the other hand, there has been increased pressure on places, partly due to the phenomenon of 'feminisation' of the senior grades of the general education school. (9)

Despite the relative decline in applicants higher education is still much valued by parents and young people. So much so that admission procedures are a perennial subject of public discussion, and the rigid entry rules give rise to quite a lot of malpractice. Occasionally one reads of the composition of admissions panels being rigged. The rule that no admissions tutor may legally serve for more than three years is widely ignored. Candidates have also been known to forge the documents they have to submit in their application or to send someone to impersonate them in the entrance examinations. And admissions tutors have frequently been influenced, pestered and indeed bribed by the parents and relatives of applicants. (10)

STUDENT CHARACTERISTICS

What sort of background does the average Soviet student come from? What are his or her socio-demographic characteristics? These are the sort of questions which have most interested both Soviet and Western observers alike. In what follows we shall focus our attention primarily on full-time students.

Age

The vast majority of Soviet full-time students are aged between 17 and 24 years. Despite the upper age limit of 35, there are very few of what Western educationists would call 'mature students'. According to a number of recent Soviet sources day students constitute some 13 per cent of all young people aged 16 to 24. (11) This statistic is actually taken from the 1970 Census so that it can hardly be applicable to present-day students, but it is the only one that Soviet scholars can call on. In the past two decades Soviet students have become younger on average. A large nationwide survey conducted by the Academy of Sciences in the seventies established that in 1969 some 44 per cent of all entrants were aged 18 years or less, but only four years later this had risen to 58 per cent. Conversely, the proportion for first-year students who were 20 years of age or more dropped from 31 per cent to 23. The survey showed that the highest proportion of very young students was to be

Table 7.3: Percentage of female students in Soviet higher education, 1970-1986

Type of Institution	Higher Education			
	1970-71	1975-76	1980-81	1985-86
All	49	50	52	55
Industry, construction, transport, communication	38	40	42	44
Agriculture	30	33	34	36
Economics, law	60	62	67	71
Medicine, physical education and sport	56	56	58	60
Education, art, cinematography	66	68	69	74
USSR population	53.9	53.5	53.3	53.0

Source: <u>Narodnoe khozyaistvo SSSR v 1985 g.</u> (Finansy i statistika, Moscow, 1986), pp. 6, 517.

found in major urban centres such as Moscow, Sverdlovsk and Novosibirsk. In the last-named city, location of the well-known Akademgorodok, precociousness went even further with nearly half of the final-year respondents claiming to have been 17 or under on entry. (12) Since then this trend has continued. (13)

Sex

Reference was made above to the phenomenon of 'feminisation' of the upper classes of the general education school. To some extent it is also to be found in higher education. Overall women are slightly overrepresented in Soviet VUZs - 55 per cent as against 53 per cent in the population at large (see Table 7.3). But there exist clear traditional imbalances as between fields of study. Thus, typically 7 out of 10 students in education, economics, law and fine arts institutes are women, and 6 out of 10 in the case of medicine. This pattern of representation has been found in surveys of students in other East European countries. (14) There is some evidence too that men studying in what might be called the 'female' disciplines such as education and medicine do not stay the course as well as women. And in the same way women appear to fare less well between the first and final years of courses in economics and agriculture. In engineering and technology, however, though underrepresented, women manage to hold their own. (15)

Previous schooling

The educational background of Soviet students follows a predictable pattern. As in Britain most of them enter full-time higher education straight from school; about three-quarters, in fact. And almost all of these complete their secondary education in a general education school rather than in a vocational-technical school, technical college or evening (shift) school. A sizeable group has previously attended special boarding schools, or specialised classes within general schools where they received advanced tuition. (16) According to the All-Union Survey in the 1970s as many as one in four of students in Moscow and Estonia had received this superior type of schooling. (17) There is general recognition among Soviet parents that ordinary secondary general schools cannot provide adequate preparation for VUZ entrance exams even though these exams are supposed not to go beyond the secondary school syllabuses. Most applicants, therefore, have recourse to additional coaching either on official preparatory courses run by the higher education establishments themselves or from private tutors. A cursory glance at advertising boards in the centre of many Russian cities will indicate how widespread private paid tutoring is. It is not uncommon to find that up to a quarter of successful entrants, particularly for popular courses such as humanities in the universities and medicine, have used the services of a private coach. (18)

Not only has the number of applicants dropped, but their quality has also been criticised. One is reminded indeed of the oft heard cry in Britain of 'Bring back the grammar schools!' when a prominent member of the USSR Academy of Sciences declares that the Education Reform is going wrong and that the students entering higher education have a low level of knowledge, and then goes on to suggest that instruction in the upper grades of the general school should become more specialised and more competitive. And, we learn, not only are present-day students lacking in academic knowledge, but their motivation in pursuing the specialism of their choice is also inadequate. Suffice it to say that nearly half the Soviet Union's graduate engineers, despite several years of expensive training paid for by the state, are employed in jobs where their specialised skills are not utilised. (19) The same goes for vocational orientation among graduates of the lower-level vocational training establishments. (20)

Work experience

The lowering of the average age of Soviet students is a feature of all regions of the country. Despite this, paradoxically, there has been a considerable increase in the proportion of students with work experience and of ex-national servicemen. These categories account for 16 per cent or so of the total intake of students. (21) Those with two years' work experience (stazh) are given certain concessions in admissions. More and more demobbed ex-servicemen are also being allowed to enter higher education on easier terms. Many would-be students of this type first attend so-called preparatory divisions attached to VUZs. These have provided since 1969 full-time revision courses for manual workers and peasants, as well as demobbed soldiers. At the end of the course they are guaranteed non-competitive entry into higher education proper. In this way it is hoped to give a more proletarian character to the composition of the student body. (22) Also offered easier access to VUZ courses - in order to swell numbers and meet intake targets in technological subjects - are the best graduates of vocational-technical schools and technical colleges.

Married students

Given the youthful age structure of the student population, it is not surprising that only a small number of students are married on entry. A major survey in Russia and the Baltic Republics in the late seventies found that the highest proportion was to be found among engineers and economists - about five to six per cent. (23) Other large-scale studies have traced a big rise in married students overall - from 10 per cent in 1970 to 18 per cent in 1980. Nearly half of them had children. (24) A more recent study still, confined to students at Leningrad University, found that by the final year of their course nearly one-third of students had married. (25) This finding was confirmed for VUZs in Latvia at about the same time. When asked about their attitude to marriage, two-thirds of first-year students in Leningrad declared themselves in favour of it, the men less so than the women. (26)

Curiously enough, looking at the figures for student marriage according to subject of study, it would appear that students in the more 'male' disciplines marry more readily. Geologists in Leningrad University beat the rest with 31 per cent of them married, while language students, mainly women, trailed behind with only 16 per cent. (27) Most student marriages understandably are contracted in the later years of a course. This is when the engineers and economists are caught up by the future doctors and farmers. Trainee teachers, however, presumably assiduous and single-minded about their academic studies to the end, occupy last place in the marriage stakes. (28) Not that getting married is always simply a matter of maturation in the Soviet context. Getting married has traditionally been one way of avoiding an uncongenial work assignment on graduation. But the recent trend cannot be explained by such utilitarian considerations. What seems to be a more influential motive for students is the psychological support that marriage can bring. (29)

The attitude of the higher education authorities in the past to student marriage has been simply to ignore it. Accommodation was not provided and no special financial aid made available. Few VUZ hostel places were set aside for married students and many have had to use the private sector; for students such accommodation can be rather expensive and unattractive. (30) Clandestine living by spouses and children in student hostels was therefore not unknown. However, the official approach has changed significantly in recent years, and much concern is now shown for the welfare of married students. (31) This is clearly connected with the demographic crisis that the European part of the Soviet Union is undergoing and with the pro-natalist policy of the government.

Social background

Virtually all higher education institutions are located in

cities or large towns. The British predilection for placing universities in small towns, villages, or in the middle of nowhere would make little sense, of course, in Soviet conditions. Potential students from rural areas do not have the opportunity to attend preparation courses run by VUZs or obtain coaching facilities so easily, and hence they tend to be at a disadvantage in the entrance competition. Later on, too, they experience particular problems of adaptation to urban life. But when they do eventually settle down they can perform academically as well as their counterparts from towns. The problem for the authorities often is to convince them of the need to return to the countryside to work.

The whole question of the social background of Soviet students and how it affects their access to higher education greatly preoccupied Soviet sociologists in the 1960s and 1970s. Most researchers then showed that certain social groups were more successful than others in exploiting the education system in pursuit of the final coveted goal of a VUZ place. Longitudinal studies of the career intentions of school pupils, for example, demonstrated that working-class and peasant children were much more inclined at the age of fifteen to transfer to vocational training institutions rather than stay on into the senior grades of secondary general-education school and thus follow an academic track leading more surely to higher education. (32)

The gap between standards of school tuition - geared to the average performer - and the requirements of the highly selective VUZ entry examinations has traditionally proved advantageous to candidates from more cultured and intellectual homes. So the chances lower socio-economic groups have of obtaining a higher education were (and still are) less than those of children from nonmanual backgrounds, despite the legal equality of opportunity and universal secondary education.

We have written elsewhere about this issue and the continuing debate it has provoked in the Soviet Union. (33) Since the seventies, however, Soviet sociologists and educationalists appear to have turned their attention away from concern about social inequality in education. Indeed, official figures on the social class composition of Soviet students (collected annually from VUZs by the Ministry of Higher and Secondary Specialised Education) have not been published in the 1980s, notwithstanding the recent policy of <u>glasnost</u> and strong protests about the lack of social statistics by leading Soviet academics. This is somewhat perplexing as a certain improvement in the representation of manual workers and collective farmers among entrants to VUZs had been noted through the seventies. (34) It seems unlikely that the pattern of class differences in the social composition of the student body will have altered significantly for the better in recent years. But to conclude that official silence in this matter denotes a worsening of the situation might be presumptuous. (35)

Table 7.4 presents official statistics which though irritatingly incomplete are the most recent ones published. The columns marked A lump together figures for social origins (based on father's occupation) in respect of entrants without work experience with those for the occupational status of students who entered higher education directly from employment. By comparing these percentages with the population data we can see that manual workers and collective farmers are clearly underrepresented in the 1977 intake. In 1980 there was a slight decline in the figures for both manual and nonmanual workers, while collective farmers actually reach parity with their share in the population at large.

However, many entrants claiming manual-worker status on the basis of previous employment come in reality from nonmanual backgrounds. They work for just a short time in manual occupations with the express intention of benefiting from the easier VUZ access offered to candidates with manual-work experience. This may be partly reflected in the B columns of Table 7.4 which indicate social origins alone as recorded in the annual statistical returns made by VUZs to the Ministry of Higher and Secondary Specialised Education. Here what we may term Soviet 'middle-class' children are seen to be even more overrepresented at the expense of both the other social groups.

Soviet researchers sometimes describe this situation by utilising a 'mobility coefficient' (koefitsient vykhoda). (36) Thus, if perfect representation of a social group, that is identical proportions in both general and student populations, is taken as 100 per cent, then the data in the B columns suggest that manual workers have a 79 per cent chance of obtaining a higher education, collective farm peasants a 44 per cent chance, and nonmanuals - 184 per cent, a ratio of nearly two to one. Filippov established similar quotients (but with an even higher percentage of 210 for children from nonmanual backgrounds) among a large sample of Russian and Baltic Republics students in a major

169

Table 7.4: Social composition of first-year students in VUZs by (A) former occupation and social origins, (a) and (B) social origins alone, 1977-1980 (per cent)

Socio-occupational background	USSR population 1979 Census	First-year students 1977-78		1979-80		1980-81	
		A	B	A	B	A	B
Manual worker	60.0	50.0	46.5	60.6	47.3	48.0	–
Collective-farmer	14.9	11.0	6.4		6.5	15.0	–
Nonmanual worker	25.1	(39.0)[b]	47.1	(39.4)	46.2	37.0	–
Total	100.0	100.0	100.0	100.0	100.0	100.0	

Notes:
(a) The social background of students entering higher education from employment is determined by the nature of their occupation, while the social origins of other entrants is taken from their father's occupation.
(b) Bracketed figures are obtained by subtraction.

Sources: For A columns – Byulleten Ministerstva vysshevo i srednevo spetsialnovo obrazovaniya, no. 2 (1978), p. 8; no. 4 (1980), p. 8; and no. 12 (1980), p. 8; N.F. Krasnov, 'Konstitutsionnye osnovy vysshevo obrazovaniya v SSSR,' Vestnik vysshei shkoly, no. 1 (1978), p. 5; for B columns – L. Ya. Rubina, Sovetskoe studenchestvo (Mysl, Moscow, 1981), p. 55-6; for Census data – Chislennost i sostav naseleniya SSSR (Finansy i statistika, Moscow, 1984), p. 155.

Table 7.5: Social origins of first-year students in the Russian Republic and the three Baltic Republics by type of VUZ, 1977-78 (per cent)

Father's occupation	Universities		Other VUZs				
	humanities	natural sciences	technology	agriculture	economics	education	medicine
Manual worker	32.2	31.2	40.3	30.9	32.4	39.0	26.0
Collective-farmer	3.8	5.6	5.6	33.6	3.6	13.6	2.7
Routine nonmanual	7.7	5.6	7.3	8.0	4.3	6.8	8.7
Highly-qualified nonmanual	49.2	51.5	39.9	21.4	54.1	32.8	52.1
Others and non-response	(7.1)(a)	(6.1)	(6.9)	(6.1)	(5.6)	(7.8)	(10.5)
Total	100.0	100.0	100.0	100.0	100.0	100.0	100.0

Note: (a) Bracketed figures, deliberately not included by the source, are here obtained by subtraction.

Source: F.R. Filippov 'Obrazovanie i sotsialnaya struktura,' in V.N. Ivanov (ed.), Razvitie sotsialnoi struktury obshchestva v SSSR (Nauka, Moscow, 1985), p. 135.

international survey in 1977-78. (37) When the figures in the Table are compared with data for earlier years, it becomes clear that the access of manual workers and peasants was improving slowly throughout the seventies. Nevertheless, the intractable nature of the problem of the factual inequality of educational opportunity at this level does surface from time to time among the expressed concerns of politicians and educationalists. In order to put such matters into perspective, it must be said that by comparison with the situation in advanced capitalist countries, the Soviet working class's mobility coefficient is very impressive.

Further survey data have been adduced in Table 7.5 to demonstrate that the social-class background of students differs considerably according to field of study. Here we are dealing with particular sub-samples of the student population so that we can only draw tentative conclusions. But the differences have been confirmed in numerous other smaller studies. University, medical and economics students are dominated by the Soviet middle class. Students of peasant origin go in for agriculture more than most, as one might expect, and also for education, a field in which priority in admission is given both to rural candidates - who are sent back to the countryside to work after graduation - and to males!

ACADEMIC WORK

The first-degree (diploma) courses followed by Soviet students are generally much longer and more thorough in their scope than those in British or North American universities and colleges. Most last for five years and include a period of industrial or other practical work experience. The academic teaching year in Soviet VUZs runs from the beginning of September to mid- or late June and comprises some 40 weeks of tuition and assessment spread over two semesters with just two weeks' break between them. The weekly work load of students is equally daunting by British standards. In all but the final year of their course they are required by the model regulations issued by the Ministry of Higher and Secondary Specialised Education of the USSR in 1986 to attend some 27 hours (36 'academic hours') of compulsory classes per week. (38) Quite frequently these hours are increased by individual institutions to accommodate extra subjects or to make up for teaching time sacrificed in September each year when most second-, third- and fourth-year students are officially sent to collective and state farms to help with the harvest. (39) And on top of contact hours a further 18 hours of private study are recommended. (40)

The academic life of Soviet students is subjected also to what may appear to liberal Western educationalists to be rather oppressive centralised direction and bureaucratic control. (41) All curricula, syllabuses, textbooks and other reading matter, as well as timetables and student behaviour are prescribed in great detail. Rules and regulations abound. Consider, for example, the following paragraph spelling out student responsibilities taken from the Ministry's 1986 rules for internal VUZ discipline:

20. Students ... are obliged:
(a) to master systematically and profoundly theoretical knowledge and practical skills in their chosen specialism;
(b) to master Marxist-Leninist theory and raise their ideological-political, scientific and cultural level, and to take an active part in the public life of the collective of the academic establishment;
(c) to acquire organisational skills for mass-political and upbringing work;
(d) to attend compulsory classes and to complete within the set period all types of assignment set out in curricula and syllabuses;
(e) to participate actively in socially useful labour;
(f) to oppose shortcomings and manifestations of alien morality and to adopt an active stance in life;
(g) to observe the rules for internal discipline in higher education establishments and student halls of residence. (42)

Other paragraphs smack of old-fashioned paternalism, to put it mildly: '22. When the heads of VUZ or faculty enter a lecture room, students are obliged to stand up ... 24. Students should be well-behaved and neatly dressed both within the VUZ and outside, and in public places.' (43) Moreover, discipline and control are exercised through a system of group leaders directly appointed by VUZ authorities rather than by the students themselves:

62. The dean of the faculty will appoint a leader in each academic student group from among the best and most disciplined students. The group leader is directly responsible to the dean and will carry out his instructions and directives within the group. The group leader's functions include: 1. to keep a record of each student's attendance at all classes. 2. to report daily to the dean those students who have missed or come late to classes giving reasons for such lateness. 3. to ensure academic discipline in the group during lectures and practicals and to look after teaching equipment. 4. to organise punctual receipt and distribution among students of textbooks and learning aids. 5. to control the receipt and distribution of maintenance grants to members of the group. (44)

It goes without saying that Soviet students are used to this sort of regimentation and have their own ways of coping with it.

Hitherto, the emphasis in student learning has been on the assimilation of large amounts of factual material, commentary and interpretation contained in a limited range of officially approved sources and texts. The development of independent research and powers of critical analysis based on wider reading, and of creativity and personal initiative has not traditionally been encouraged. (45) 'Straight-jacket' instruction purveyed for six hours a day, six days a week in compulsory classes, together with heavy home-assignment requirements have inevitably had a stultifying effect on student attitudes to academic work.

They have responded to these pressures by ignoring workload norms, by missing classes, reading superficially and selectively, copying each other's work, and even by cheating in examinations. (46) Soviet time-budget research, for example, has shown that the actual weekly attendance of compulsory classes by students can be ten hours on average below official norms. Typically, the researchers have not been prompted by their findings to question the norms themselves or to examine more closely student motivation or academic structures to find the causes of absenteeism. They are more inclined simply to bemoan the loss of valuable hours of instruction. (47) Even when clear evidence is provided that VUZs not infrequently increase recommended contact hours and that students cope by adopting their own priorities when organising their academic and social life, official requirements remain essentially unchallenged in recommendations arising from such research. For example, one of the most representative investigations of student time use discovered, not surprisingly, that the total number of hours over five years devoted to some VUZ courses was less than in other courses. The author, a well-known authority in this field, seems to be unduly concerned at this arithmetical inconsistency because it meant that some students get less contact hours than others. He describes it as 'squandering ... society's wealth -time.' In similar vein, when he found that on average about 63 per cent of students missed classes, resulting in a weekly loss of 2 hours and 41 minutes of compulsory class time (out of 27 hours), he expressed alarm at what he saw as evidence of faulty organisation and planning. (48)

What then are student priorities as far as academic work is concerned? The results of a number of recent large-scale sociological surveys of student opinion are representative enough to give us some broad indication. A major research project on higher education and the social structure of Soviet society conducted in the mid-seventies asked first-year students about their plans for their immediate future at VUZ. It was discovered that at the outset of their course most Soviet students are intent on 'enjoying the benefits of student life' (68 per cent). 'Devoting oneself to academic studies' comes second but figures in the plans of only 45 per cent of respondents. And this was closely followed by 'enjoying a fuller cultural life' which 40 per cent had in mind; indeed, this response appeared to be more popular than devotion to study among university humanities students (56 per cent) and trainee teachers (58 per cent). (49)

These data might be dismissed as the immature perceptions of freshers, except that the broad pattern of response to this item in the survey tended to be confirmed in later studies which involved final-year students as well. For example, students from VUZs in the Russian Federal Republic and the Baltic Republics taking part in an international survey in 1978-79 were asked to state the degree of importance they attached to various activities. As can be seen in Table 7.6, in their overall ranking academic study comes third after social and cultural activities. Indeed, almost one-third of the Russian sample were prepared to admit that their studies were of no great

Table 7.6: Student views on the importance of various activities, Russian Federation and Baltic Republics, 1977-1979

| Type of activity (and overall ranking)* | Degree of importance (% of students) | | | | | | | |
| | Very great | | Fairly great | | Not very great | | Insignificant | |
	Russia	Baltic	Russia	Baltic	Russia	Baltic	Russia	Baltic
Academic study to master specialism (3)	23.9	45.7	37.4	43.6	16.2	9.8	15.3	0.9
Socio-political work (6)	7.3	11.0	25.3	39.5	37.2	40.9	23.9	8.6
Being with friends (1)	32.1	50.2	43.1	42.1	14.6	7.2	3.3	0.6
Hobbies (4)	14.6	35.7	27.3	40.4	31.3	19.9	21.7	4.0
Sport (7)	9.1	25.0	21.3	36.4	28.4	31.7	40.3	6.9
Theatres, concerts, exhibitions, reading (2)	29.7	45.0	38.0	44.7	25.9	9.6	5.3	0.7
Boyfriend/girlfriend	-	55.9	-	29.0	-	9.6	-	5.5
Family life (5)	23.9	-	17.0	-	11.0	-	36.9	-

*Note: Overall ranking is based on the combined percentages of the columns 'very great' and 'fairly great', and refers here to Russian students only. The ranking of the Baltic students' responses is essentially the same.

Source: F.R. Filippov and P.E. Mitev (eds), Molodyozh i vysshee obrazovanie v sotsialisticheskikh stranakh, (Nauka, Moscow, 1984), p. 115.

importance at all. And in answer to another section of the questionnaire (not shown in the Table) almost one-fifth of them similarly regarded raising their educational level and acquiring vocational skills - fundamental aims of all Soviet higher education - as of little importance. The authors of the survey see this as an example of what they term the 'passivity' of many of the Russian students which they excuse by the irrelevant but revealing comment that a lot of the sample was drawn from provincial VUZs of Russia! (50)

Attitudes such as these are reflected in actual work patterns. A large survey in the early eighties found that only just over a quarter of students claimed to study systematically. Most - nearly two-thirds - worked 'from time to time', while eleven per cent admitted to doing scarcely any academic work at all. (51) When they organise their studies, the activity which almost all students spend a great deal of time on is revising for examinations and tests. But day-to-day preparation for seminars gets but scant attention from nearly 50 per cent of students. Instead, they seem to prefer reading fiction. These were the conclusions, too, of another major survey of the late seventies conducted by Leningrad sociologists among over 4000 students in 18 VUZs in various parts of the Soviet Union (see Table 7.7). Furthermore, the data in the Table suggest that other academic reading, socio-political work and research - all considered especially important and worthy from an official point of view - are less favoured than television watching, relaxing with friends and informal socialising.

Frequent reference is made by Soviet academics and educational commentators to the passive, superficial and unprofessional attitudes to their academic obligations displayed by students. (52) In fact, criticism of students coupled with invidious comparisons with their idealistic and enthusiastic predecessors in the heroic decades of Soviet history has been a feature of much writing on higher education. Even the Party Central Committee at its Plenary Session held in June 1983 attacked 'the immature civic consciousness and political naivety, dependence on others and refusal to work where modern society required' which characterise some young people and students. (53) The hard line here is perhaps epitomised in a recent article by the leading sociologist, M. Rutkevich, on the current reforms in secondary and higher education:

The prohibition on retaking examinations from the past

Table 7.7: Student time use by type of activity

Type of activity (and overall ranking)*	Amount of time spent on activity (% of students)			
	Very much	Much	Little	Very Little
Preparation for examinations and tests (1)	37.9	46.0	14.2	1.9
Reading fiction (2)	25.9	44.6	24.3	5.2
Watching television and listening to radio (4)	7.4	36.1	41.6	14.9
Reading and preparation for seminars (3)	6.6	44.4	37.9	11.1
Hobbies and creative activities (7)	6.5	19.5	38.2	35.8
Participation in sport (12)	5.3	12.9	31.0	50.8
Socio-political activities (9)	4.5	20.6	37.7	37.2
Student research work (10)	4.4	16.8	24.2	54.6
Relaxing with friends, informal social life, dancing (5)	3.6	25.5	49.0	21.9
Reading socio-political literature (newspapers, journals, attending lectures on foreign and domestic affairs) (6)	3.6	23.4	53.5	19.5

Table 7.7: continued

Type of activity (and overall ranking)*	Amount of time spent on activity (% of students)			
	Very much	Much	Little	Very Little
Going to theatre, concerts and exhibitions (8)	2.5	23.1	54.7	19.7
Amateur artistic performance (14)	2.2	6.3	11.9	79.6
Watching sport (11)	2.1	19.0	19.0	59.9
Reading philosophical literature (13)	2.1	7.9	33.6	56.4

*Note: Overall ranking is based on the combined percentages of the columns 'very much' and 'much'.

Source: V.T. Lisovsky (ed.), Obraz zhizni sovremennovo studenta: sotsiologicheskoe issledovanie (Leningrad State University, Leningrad, 1981), p. 127.

179

academic year and the expulsion of all remiss students, without reducing the size of the teaching staff, will undoubtedly make it possible to increase exactingness and to stop the practice of dragging future mediocre specialists to the state examinations 'by the ears' ... all those who cannot or do not want to study as hard as possible must be removed from the higher schools without any compunction. (54)

Many observers, however, acknowledge now that the traditional timetable and teaching methods, and the excessive demands made upon students can be counterproductive. (55) Leonavichyus has demonstrated how the amount of reading prescribed in the social science subjects is outrageously excessive for the amount of time allocated for it. '(For a student to be able) to read, annotate and assimilate 266, 141 or 94 pages of set literature in the 90 minutes (allotted to it) is impossible.' (56) In one striking experiment a Moscow VUZ rector asked his senior staff themselves to undertake all the reading and other assignments that their students were expected to complete in one week's private study. It took these experienced Soviet dons between 80 and 90 hours to accomplish this task. (57) Yet the recommended weekly norm for student private study is 18 hours.

STUDENT FREE TIME

When it comes to students' leisure time, then Soviet pedagogues and ideologues quite emphatically think it should be organised on rational lines and filled with activities which they (the pedagogues and ideologues) deem to be necessary or good for them. A different response, naturally, comes from students when they have been asked how they actually utilise their spare time. As we have noted in Tables 7.6 and 7.7 above, by far the most popular leisure-time interests of Soviet students are reading fiction and watching television, followed by relaxing and going out with friends. That is, predominantly passive and spontaneous activities. Active pursuits such as amateur theatricals and sport are engaged in by only a small number of enthusiasts. More recent research supports these general findings. (58) Soviet researchers in this area of student life, however, seem to feel compelled to bemoan the fact that activities like

reading fiction occupy a more important place in the time
budget of respondents than preparing for seminars or doing
research work. For instance, in the view of the Leningrad
sociologists, the 'lot of time' that 43.5 per cent of the
students devote to TV viewing is a waste. It could, after all,
be used for doing more academic work on one's own. (59)
Other commentators, more realistically, point out that
leisure time has a restorative function and that relaxation
and passive activities can actually help in maintaining the
productivity of work time proper. (60)

Still, when young people do indulge in casual socialising
with friends, Soviet sociologists have thought it important
to find out what they actually get up to. And it turns out,
mirabile dictu, that Soviet students like to enjoy
themselves, to go dancing, celebrate birthdays, have heart-
to-heart talks about personal and intimate affairs, or just
talk shop. At least that is what students said in a survey
carried out in Kaliningrad and they surely cannot be so
different from students elsewhere in the Soviet Union, or in
the world, for that matter. (61)

Such normal leisure activities of Soviet student youth
evoke no surprise. But our usual notions about Soviet
behaviour might receive something of a shock when we find
out from the sociologists what they do not do. We are not
referring here to the fact that a large proportion of students
turn their back on active pursuits such as sport and artistic
performance. It is rather evidence of apparent lack of
cultural interests which amazes. For example, a most
unexpected (for Western observers only, perhaps) finding of
the major survey in 18 VUZs mentioned above was that 25
per cent of students had never been to the theatre in the
course of the year, 58 per cent had never been to opera or
ballet, 66 per cent had never attended a concert of classical
music, and 19 per cent had never been to a museum or art
exhibition! (62)

STUDENT DROPOUT

The day of reckoning comes in the lives of a certain number
of students; those who are expelled for failing their
examinations or for non-attendance and the like, or for
violating public order. Wastage necessarily poses a serious
problem to a higher education system which is part and
parcel of a planned economy. Something like 30 per cent of

all Soviet students do not finish their course on time for one reason or another over the five years of a typical course. For full-time students the figure is more like one-third of this. (63) The overwhelming majority of dropouts are male students who leave in the first two years of the course. In Leningrad University two-thirds of all wastage was found to be due to academic failure and transfers and a further 11 per cent simply did not want to continue studying. (64) (It must be said here that a lot more may have also lost interest in their course but did not leave it.) Some six per cent were expelled for 'infringement of academic discipline', that is missing lectures, failing to take examinations, or cheating. And another four per cent or so for public order offences. (65) The latter reasons obviously much concern the University authorities, since they regard them as disturbing evidence of moral laxity, which calls for 'a strengthening of upbringing work' and tighter selection procedures. When first-year students are expelled for these reasons, some or all of the blame can be put on their previous upbringing at school or in the home. But when the data show that things are worse in years 4 and 5 of the course, the same excuse cannot be made. (66) As far as family background of dropouts goes, it seems to be the sons of highly-qualified nonmanual parents, 'the golden youth' or 'hooray Ivans' who are the worst offenders. (67)

IDEOLOGICAL TRAINING

All Soviet students are obliged to take, in addition to their main subjects, social science courses in Marxist-Leninist Philosophy, History of the Communist Party of the Soviet Union, Political Economy, and Scientific Communism. This ideological training is considered essential for the future activists and leaders in Soviet society. But again students seem not to share this view. This was particularly apparent from their half-hearted attitudes to and participation in socio-political work - a good practical measure of the efficacy of social science teaching (see Tables 7.6 and 7.7).

The most recent empirical demonstration of this came in an extensive survey of student opinion in several large cities throughout the Soviet Union in autumn 1986. (68) A team of researchers from the Academy of Sciences' Institute of Sociological Research questioned 1657 full-time students on their attitudes to the teaching of their social science courses. The survey showed that students performed well in examinations in these subjects, but displayed insufficient genuine interest and involvement. Thus, only 25 per cent participated actively in seminars, 31 per cent produced written work for social science competitions and just 21 per cent did any wider reading beyond the set texts. Many respondents were just concerned with recording a pass in the examinations. (69) One-third of them failed to appreciate the value of studying the social sciences for developing a correct world outlook; nearly a quarter thought Marxist-Leninist theory irrelevant for a future graduate's career. Just over a quarter (but only six per cent of engineering students) claimed to be positively interested and actively involved in their social science studies. (70) The majority, however, in the eyes of the researchers, seemed merely to pay lip-service to the notion that Marxism-Leninism was important for them because they proved incapable of formulating for themselves a view on social affairs and of defending it. (71) And then there was a hard core of about 19 to 22 per cent who expressed a consistently negative attitude to this part of their academic work and refused to take any part in seminars. Among the latter were 32 per cent of engineers, 26 per cent of medical students and as many as 40 per cent of students of the applied arts. (72)

In the evaluation of lectures in the social sciences, responses differed clearly according to type of VUZ, but most students obviously viewed them as irrelevant to their chosen careers. (73) The same dismissive attitude was found in relation to private reading of social science materials. As many as 43 per cent thought it not important in developing a world outlook, and 20 per cent did no such reading at all. (74) It comes as no surprise when the researchers conclude that social science teachers in VUZs do not enjoy general popularity. (75)

Not that a proper scientific world outlook was considered unimportant for a successful professional life - four-fifths of the sample agreed that it was. But in their scale of factors which determine the quality of a higher education the development of such an outlook occupies a low rank. And as for making use of their social science knowledge in their future work, this intention was lacking in virtually all the students surveyed. (76) Conformity in words but not in action is one of the negative features of Soviet life which Gorbachov is attempting to overcome with his policy of glasnost as a part of perestroika. It was dismaying, therefore, for the researchers to record the above results and to finish by revealing that when it comes to implementing perestroika only 37 per cent of the nation's future elite declared themselves prepared to do so. (77)

CONCLUSION

The evidence we have adduced above makes it clear that from the student's point of view Soviet VUZs have been failing for some time in their primary academic function. Students have generally shown a decided lack of enthusiasm for the teaching they receive. What is more, their disillusion seems to increase the more they progress through their course. (78) Negative attitudes to VUZ education have no doubt contributed to a widespread deterioration in the professional orientation and ideological conviction of Soviet students which has caused great official concern in recent years. (79) It is after all the fundamental purpose of Soviet higher education to prepare the nation's most talented young people for specialised occupational roles and for political and social leadership. Too many students, however, lose interest in their specialism and after graduation abandon the professions for which they have been trained at great cost to the state. And too many are dismayed by the gulf which they readily perceive between the Marxist-Leninist theory and scientific communism they are taught on the one hand, and the realities of Soviet life on the other.

What proposals do students themselves make to remedy this state of affairs? Given the powers of a faculty dean, what changes would they introduce to correct poor teaching methods and mediocre performance? This question was put to large samples of students in 1978-79 and in 1982-83. On both occasions the same sort of suggestions were made: 'cut down the number of compulsory classes', 'be firmer with students and make them more responsible for their studies', 'expel layabouts' said the hard-liners, 'bring in more options', 'make lectures voluntary', 'change the system of teaching radically' and 'sack staff who read their lectures from textbooks!' (80) The smell of revolution? Well, just a few years after these surveys in the spring of 1987 many of those suggestions have found their way into the Party's basic guidelines for a radical reform of the country's higher education system. (81) And from now on it is intended that the voice of students will really be listened to as they take on a major role in the running of their own VUZs.

NOTES

1.   VUZ is an acronym from the Russian vysshee uchebnoe zavedenie (higher education establishment). According to normal convention it will be used hereafter in both nominal and adjectival senses.

2.   Byulleten Ministerstva vysshevo i srednevo spetsialnovo obrazovaniya SSSR (MV i SSO), no. 6 (1987), pp. 2, 14, and no. 8 (1987), pp. 2-4.

3.   For complaints by Soviet scholars about the lack of official statistical information see, for example, Sotsiologicheskie issledovaniya, no. 1 (1987), pp. 132-3, 139; Vestnik vysshei shkoly, no. 12 (1986), p. 74.

4.   Narodnoe khozyaistvo SSSR v 1985 g. (Finansy i statistika, Moscow, 1986), p. 508.

5.   F.R. Filippov and V.A. Malova, 'O nekotorykh napravleniyakh povysheniya effektivnosti obrazovaniya,' Sotsiologicheskie issledovaniya, no. 2 (1984), p. 65.

6.   Byulleten MV i SSO, no. 11 (1984), p. 7.

7.   The swing from higher education, especially in respect of technological subjects, is well documented. See, for example, I.S. Bolotin, 'Vozdeistvie demograficheskoi situatsii na srednyuyu i vysshuyu shkoly,' Sotsiologicheskie issledovaniya, no. 4 (1979), pp. 127-8; O. Karpukhin and V. Kutsenko, Student sevodnya - spetsialist zavtra (Molodaya gvardiya, Moscow, 1983), pp. 44-9.

8.   Byulleten MV i SSO, no. 11 (1984), pp. 6-7.

9.   S.N. Tvorogov, 'Istochniki komplektovaniya studencheskovo sostava,' Vestnik vysshei shkoly, no. 5 (1983), pp. 8-12; G. Avis, 'Access to higher education in the Soviet Union' in J. Tomiak (ed), Soviet Education in the 1980s (Croom Helm, London, 1983), pp. 203-8.

10.   See, for example, Byulleten MV i SSO, no. 6 (1983), p. 4, and no. 9 (1986), pp. 4-6.

11.   For example, see V.T. Lisovsky and V.A. Sukhin (eds), Kompleksnoe issledovanie problem obucheniya i kommunisticheskovo vospitaniya spetsialistov s vysshim obrazovaniem (Leningrad University, Leningrad, 1980), p. 10.

12.   M.N. Rutkevich and F.R. Filippov (eds), Vysshaya shkola kak faktor sotsialnoi struktury razvitovo

sotsialisticheskovo obshchestva (Nauka, Moscow, 1978), pp. 128, 149.

13. L. Ya. Rubina, 'Tendentsii izmeneniya sotsialnovo sostava studenchestva (na materialakh vuzov g. Sverdlovska),' in V.A. Malova (ed.), Sotsialnaya effektivnost obrazovaniya (USSR Academy of Sciences, Institute of Sociological Research, Moscow, 1983), p. 74.

14. F.R. Filippov and P.E. Mitev (eds), Molodyozh i vysshee obrazovanie v sotsialisticheskikh stranakh (Nauka, Moscow, 1984), p. 79.

15. Avis, 'Access to higher education,' p. 208.

16. Rutkevich and Filippov (eds), Vysshaya shkola kak faktor, p. 129.

17. Ibid., p. 151.

18. At a recent round-table discussion on youth organised by two serious Soviet academic journals, it was stated that two billion rubles annually are spent on private coaching in the Soviet Union (Sotsiologicheskie issledovaniya, no. 2 (1987), p. 27).

19. M.N. Rutkevich, 'Is the school reform another "mistake"?,' Current Digest of the Soviet Press, vol. 38, no. 47 (1986), p. 3.

20. Filippov and Malova, 'O nekotorykh napravleniyakh,' p. 65.

21. Rutkevich and Filippov (eds), Vysshaya shkola kak faktor, p. 127.

22. See G. Avis, 'Preparatory divisions in Soviet higher education establishments 1969-79: ten years of radical experiment,' Soviet Studies, vol. 35, no. 1 (January, 1983), pp. 14-35.

23. Filippov and Mitev (eds), Molodyozh i vysshee obrazovanie, p. 81.

24. T.G. Pospelova, 'Ustanovki studencheskoi molodyozhi v sfere semyi i braka,' in I.I. Eliseeva (ed.), Sotsialno-demografichesky portret studenta (Mysl, Moscow, 1986), p. 46.

25. Ibid.

26. Ibid., p. 47.

27. Ibid., p. 48.

28. Filippov and Mitev (eds), Molodyozh i vysshee obrazovanie, pp. 80-1.

29. Pospelova, 'Ustanovki studencheskoi molodyozhi,' p. 48.

30. See Byulleten MV i SSO, no. 3 (1986), p. 41.

31. Byulleten MV i SSO, no. 2 (1986), p. 30, no. 11

(1986), p. 28, and no. 5 (1987), p. 28.
 32. For a review of this evidence see G.H. Avis, 'Social class and access to full-time higher education in the Soviet Union,' unpublished MSc dissertation, University of Bradford, 1977.
 33. Ibid.; Avis, 'Access to higher education,' in Tomiak (ed.), Soviet Education in the 1980s, pp. 217-28.
 34. Avis, 'Access to higher education' in Tomiak (ed.), Soviet Education in the 1980s, pp. 219-25.
 35. In fact, official data published after this was written show a sharp drop in working-class students.
 36. For example, see Filippov and Mitev (eds), Molodyozh i vysshee obrazovanie, p. 25.
 37. F.R. Filippov, 'Obrazovanie i sotsialnaya struktura,' in V.N. Ivanov (ed.), Razvitie sotsialnoi struktury obshchestva v SSSR (aktualnye problemy sotsiologicheskikh issledovaniy) (Nauka, Moscow, 1985), p. 134.
 38. Byulleten MV i SSO, no. 6 (1986), p. 19.
 39. Yu. I. Leonavichyus, Problemy sovershenstvovaniya issledovaniya uchebnovo i vneuchebnovo fonda vremeni studentov vuzov (na materialakh sotsiologicheskikh issledovaniy v vuzakh strany), abstract of doctoral dissertation (USSR Academy of Sciences, Moscow, 1984), p. 24.
 40. A.N. Rodny, 'Byudzhet vremeni i svobodnoe vremya sovetskoi molodyozhi (Obzor),' in Ya. M. Berger (ed.), Molodyozh i svobodnoe vremya pri sotsializme: referativny sbornik (USSR Academy of Sciences, Moscow, 1984), p. 131.
 41. In response to a jibe made at a conference in October 1986 by Party Central Committee Secretary, F. Ligachov, to the effect that the bureaucracy of the Ministry of Higher Education was a main culprit in creating unnecessary paperwork, the Minister, Yagodin, pointed out that in 1985 the Ministry had received more decrees and directives from above than it had sent out itself - 1323 as against 994! (Vestnik vysshei shkoly, no. 12 (1986), pp. 18-9, 33).
 42. Byulleten MV i SSO, no. 6 (1986), p. 13.
 43. Ibid.
 44. Ibid., p. 20.
 45. For recent criticism of traditional teaching approaches see Yu. I. Leonavichyus, 'Kak sberech vremya studentov?,' Vestnik vysshei shkoly, no. 8 (1987), pp. 33-4.
 46. Rodny, 'Byudzhet vremeni,' pp. 131-2;

Leonavichyus, 'Kak sberech,' pp. 34-5; Sotsiologicheskie issledovaniya, no. 4 (1987), pp. 25-6; S.B. Nekhoroshkov, 'Osnovy formirovaniya budushchevo spetsialista,' in Eliseeva (ed.), Sotsialno-demografichesky portret, p. 36; Vestnik vysshei shkoly, no. 12 (1986), p. 62; G. Avis, 'Soviet students: lifestyle and attitudes,' in J. Dunstan (ed.), Soviet Education Under Scrutiny (Jordanhill College, Glasgow, 1987), pp. 93-7.

47. For example, see Rodny, 'Byudzhet vremeni,' pp. 131-2.

48. Leonavichyus, 'Kak sberech,' pp. 35-7.

49. L. Ya. Rubina, Sovetskoe studenchestvo (Mysl, Moscow, 1981), p. 91.

50. Filippov and Mitev (eds), Molodyozh i vysshee obrazovanie, pp. 95-6.

51. V.T. Lisovsky, 'Sotsialny i nravstvenny portret sovremennovo studenta,' in Eliseeva (ed.), Sotsialno-demografichesky portret, p. 9.

52. Ibid., pp. 10-11; Avis, 'Soviet students,' pp. 93-4; Vestnik vysshei shkoly, no. 6 (1986), p. 29.

53. Cited in Lisovsky, 'Sotsialny i nravstvenny portret,' p. 11.

54. Rutkevich, 'Is the school reform another "mistake"?,' p. 3.

55. See the speech by the Minister of Higher Education, G. Yagodin, in Vestnik vysshei shkoly, no. 12 (1986), pp. 24-6; Leonavichyus, 'Kak sberech,' pp. 33-4; Sotsiologicheskie issledovaniya, no. 4 (1987), pp. 21, 25-7.

56. Leonavichyus, 'Problemy sovershenstvovaniya,' p. 23.

57. V.T. Lisovsky, 'Obraz zhizni i tipologizatsiya studentov,' in V.T. Lisovsky (ed.), Obraz zhizni sovremennovo studenta: sotsiologicheskoe issledovanie (Leningrad University, Leningrad, 1981), p. 183.

58. For example, see Rodny, 'Byudzhet vremeni,' p. 132; Lisovsky, 'Obraz zhizni i tipologizatsia studentov,' pp. 179-80; B.A. Tregubov, 'Tsennostnye orientatsii studencheskoi molodyozhi i svobodnoe vremya,' in Lisovsky (ed.), Obraz zhizni sovremennovo studenta, pp. 130-44.

59. V.I. Kulagina, 'Byudzhet vremeni i raspredelenie vidov zhiznedeyatelnosti studentov,' in Lisovsky (ed.), Obraz zhizni sovremennovo studenta, p. 129; see also Leonvichyus, Problemy sovershenstvovaniya, pp. 35-6.

60. Ibid.; Rodny, 'Byudzhet vremeni,' p. 133.

61. Tregubov, 'Tsennostnye orientatsii,' pp. 136-7.

62. Ibid., p. 133; Lisovsky, 'Obraz zhizni i tipologizatsia studentov,' p. 191.

63. A.A. Kozlov and S.A. Medvedskaya, 'Otsev iz vuza i problema vklyucheniya studentov v protsessy vuzovskoi zhiznedeyatelnosti,' in Lisovsky (ed.), Obraz zhizni sovremennovo studenta, p. 71. These figures refer mainly to the late sixties and seventies. Ministry of Higher Education figures for net dropout in 1980-81 gives an annual rate of 4.4 per cent for all forms of higher education, including 3.1 per cent for full-time students, 8.6 per cent for evening students, and 5.1 per cent for correspondence students (Byulleten MV i SSO, no. 5 (1982), p. 8).

64. Kozlov and Medvedskaya, 'Otsev iz vuza,' pp. 72-3, 77.

65. Ibid., p. 73.

66. Ibid., pp. 76-7.

67. Ibid., pp. 78-9.

68. E.P. Vasileva et al, 'Otnoshenie studentov k obshchestvennym naukam,' Sotsiologicheskie issledovaniya, no. 4 (1987), pp. 20-4.

69. Ibid., pp. 20-1.

70. Ibid,. pp. 21-2.

71. Ibid., p. 21.

72. Ibid., pp. 21-2.

73. Ibid., p. 22.

74. Ibid.

75. Ibid., p. 24.

76. Ibid.

77. Ibid.

78. See, for example, Avis, 'Soviet students,' pp. 102-4, 109-10.

79. Ibid., pp. 98-106.

80. Lisovsky, 'Obraz zhizni i tipologizatsia studentov,' p. 186; Lisovsky, 'Sotsialny i nravstvenny portret,' pp. 9-10.

81. Izvestiya, 21 March 1987.

INDEX

Academy of Pedagogical
  Sciences of the USSR 32,
  43, 44, 47, 48, 51, 52, 144
amateurism 96, 97
America 6, 23, 70, 82, 99,
  118, 127, 136
Anderson, B.A. 83, 84
Andropov, Yu. 48
Armenia 77, 78, 80, 81, 86,
  87, 91, 92, 93, 150
art vii, 6, 13, 15, 95
atheism 9
Aubrey, C. 70
auxiliary schools 77, 78, 82,
  86, 87, 140, 149

ballet vii, 99, 118
  schools 95, 112
Baltic Republics 37, 83, 84,
  150, 166, 169, 171, 176
Bauman Institute 162
Belorussia 5, 6, 84, 86, 107
Bertyn 128
Birman, Prof. 115
birth rate 5, 45
blind children 77, 122, 134
braille 86, 127, 134
Brezhnev, L. 159
Britain (comparisons with)
  1, 11, 26, 75, 79, 80, 81,

91, 92, 95, 96, 99, 118, 122,
  127, 133, 134, 136, 140,
  147, 149, 152, 154, 155,
  161, 165, 168, 172
Burt, C. 75

catching-up classes 150, 151
Census (1979) 158, 163
Central Asia 4, 83, 84, 86,
  111
Central Music School
  (Moscow) 57
central nervous system 141,
  146, 147
Centre Internationale de
  Recherche (Paris) 41
cerebral palsy 80
character education 39, 40
Chernenko, K. 48
Chernyshevsky, N. 97
chess 112
child development 71, 72, 73
children's homes 78
China 95, 117
collective 6, 7, 134, 135
Communist Party 2, 12, 48,
  61, 157, 177, 182, 184
computer studies 22, 35, 49
conductive education vi
corruption and bribery 8, 61